AFTER THE BADGE

AFTER THE BADGE:
A TRUE STORY OF LOVE, FAITH—AND HOPE FOLLOWING LOSS

Copyright © 2021 by Owen-Speed Consulting
Published by Owen-Speed Publishers

All rights reserved. No part of this publication may be reproduced, distributed, or transmitted in any form or by any means, including photocopying, recording, or other electronic or mechanical methods, without the prior written permission from Owen-Speed Consulting, except in the case of brief quotations embodied in critical reviews and certain other noncommercial uses permitted by copyright law. For permission requests contact the publisher at info@vickieandtania.com.

Ordering Information: Quantity sales. Special discounts are available on quantity purchases by corporations, associations, and others. For details, contact the publisher at info@vickieandtania.com.

Unless otherwise noted, all Scripture quotations are taken from the NEW KING JAMES VERSION®. Copyright © 2005 by Thomas Nelson, Inc. Used by permission. All rights reserved.

Scripture marked AMPC are taken from the AMPLIFIED® BIBLE (AMPC), Copyright © 1954, 1958, 1962, 1964, 1965, 1987 by the Lockman Foundation. Used by Permission. (www.Lockman.org)

Scripture quotations marked EHV are from the Holy Bible, Evangelical Heritage Version ® (EHV ®) Copyright © Wartburg Project, Inc. All rights reserved. Used by permission.

Scriptures marked NIV are taken from the NEW INTERNATIONAL VERSION (NIV):
Scripture taken from THE HOLY BIBLE, NEW INTERNATIONAL VERSION®. Copyright © 1973, 1978, 1984, 2011 by Biblica, Inc.TM. Used by permission of Zondervan

Scriptures marked NLT are taken from the HOLY BIBLE, NEW LIVING TRANSLATION (NLT): Scriptures taken from the HOLY BIBLE, NEW LIVING TRANSLATION, Copyright © 1996, 2004, 2007 by Tyndale House Foundation. Used by permission of Tyndale House Publishers, Inc., Carol Stream, Illinois 60188. All rights reserved. Used by permission.

Vision

Produced for Owen-Speed Publishers by Vision Book Producers (VisionBookProducers.com)
Managing editor: Stacie L. Jennings; Cover and interior design: LynnCreative
Cover photography: Schlick Art Photography | Video (SchlickArt.com)

ISBN 978-1-7358979-2-9 (softcover)
ISBN 978-1-7358979-4-3 (ebook)

Printed in the United States of America

TANIA OWEN AND VICKIE SPEED

AFTER THE BADGE

A TRUE STORY OF LOVE, FAITH—AND HOPE FOLLOWING LOSS

DEDICATION

We dedicate this book to two of the greatest men we have ever known. *Steve Owen and Mitch Speed:* We are stronger, better women because of the love you showed us and the beautiful lives you gave us.

To our children: We have learned so much about perseverance, strength, and love of family because of you. You have encouraged us every step of the way.

Millie Owen and Barbara Speed: Thank you for raising such incredible sons. Steve and Mitch were raised by two strong women whose beliefs were God and family, and we are honored they chose us to be their wives.

FROM THE AUTHORS

*Blessed are the peacemakers, for they
shall be called children of God.*

MATTHEW 5:9

In a series of blessings declared in His Sermon on the Mount, Jesus identified eight specific life values that mark His followers as "the salt of the earth" and "the light of the world." Having served in law enforcement for more than three decades, I'm confident in saying that the majority of deputies and officers see themselves as the peacemakers Jesus described in Matthew 5:9. For these men and women, law enforcement is more than a career; law enforcement is a calling to serve, protect, and be a blessing in people's lives. Ultimately to stand between good and evil.

A small percentage of these professionals, however, fail to uphold their oaths to ensure the safety of all who live in the communities they serve. The public does not want such individuals serving in law enforcement, and neither do law-abiding law enforcement officers. Sadly, the media is all too often complicit in driving a divisive narrative designed to promote an agenda that has nothing to do with law enforcement.

In a time when all we have to do is turn on the evening news to see the strife and division in our country played out on our big-screen televisions, many ask, "Is there a solution to our nation's seemingly overwhelming problems?" I believe the answer is yes, for the Bible says, *"If My people who are called by my name will humble themselves, and pray and seek My face, and turn from their wicked ways, then I will hear from heaven, and will forgive their sin and heal their land"* (2 Chronicles 7:14).

I've learned that, with God, nothing is impossible.

Tania Owen, *Los Angeles County Sheriff's Department Detective (Retired); wife of Los Angeles County Sheriff's Department Sergeant Steve Owen*

FROM THE AUTHORS

Our husbands, Sergeant Steve Owen and Detective Mitch Speed, were part of the 99 percent of deputies and officers who don't choose law enforcement for notoriety, acknowledgement, or a pat on the back. These two men willingly spent time in the trenches, helping those discarded by society to find hope, stability, and a way back.

On their own time Steve and Mitch often followed up with criminals and others they'd encountered during the arrest process, sharing their faith and mentoring young men and women who desperately needed to know someone believed in them. Steve Owen and Mitch Speed changed our community for the better—one person at a time. Their work in Los Angeles County exemplifies the character of 99 percent of law enforcement personnel in our country today, yet this is not a story the media tells.

Though law enforcement marriages and families may be accustomed to the pressure that comes with the job, they are not immune to it. Our stories prove this fact. Tania and I have written this book to provide a public window into our private lives for the purpose of bringing understanding, healing, and hope to others. Most importantly, we want our stories to encourage and strengthen law enforcement marriages and families so that they may continue to be the effective peacemakers they are called to be.

Vickie Speed, *wife of Los Angeles County Sheriff's Department Detective Mitch Speed*

Contents

Dedication	v
From the Authors	vii

Part One: The Events That Changed Our Lives

1: Wednesday, October 5, 2016	15
2: A Very Public Goodbye	35
3: March 2016	51
4: The Bucket List	75
5: God Brought Me You	105

Part Two: The Good, the Bad, and the Really Bad

6: Life in the Antelope Valley	129
7: The Rest of the Journey	143
8: From El Salvador to California to Law Enforcement	159
9: Beautiful Restoration	175

Part Three: Aftermath

10: First Steps Forward	201
11: A Foundation of Faith and Love	213
12: Finding My New Normal	223
13: Blessings in the Midst of Trials	237
Epilogue: Tania and Vickie	255

Bonus Content: Poem and Essay by Mitch Speed

Death	261
Your Final Thirty Minutes	263
Acknowledgements	269

Part One

THE EVENTS THAT CHANGED OUR LIVES

"These things I have spoken to you, that in Me you may have peace. In the world you will have tribulation; but be of good cheer, I have overcome the world."

JOHN 16:33

Chapter One

WEDNESDAY, OCTOBER 5, 2016

Tania Owen

As I guided my truck down our long driveway and turned into the street, I lowered the window so that Tank could enjoy the morning air before we merged onto the highway for the 135-mile drive southeast to Palm Springs from our home in Lancaster, California.

I'd had a number of partners throughout my thirty-year career as a deputy with the Los Angeles County Sheriff's Department, but Tank was the first with four legs. The eighteen-month-old black Labrador retriever and I had recently completed our six weeks of initial training, with me as his first handler. Today we were on our way to undergo the first of three days of testing, after which Tank would officially join me as a K9 member of the bomb squad.

Tank had come into our home in July, and though he bonded beautifully with me as his partner and human mother, he had plenty of room in his heart for my husband, Steve, and daughter Shannon, a college student and the last of our three children still living at home. With the family, Tank was gentle and loving, yet he was a beast of a bomb dog—focused, determined, and committed to his job.

Shannon was still sleeping when I rose early to feed Tank and prepare for the day. Since I wouldn't return until evening, Steve, also a member of the LASD, had risen quietly several hours earlier to work an overtime shift as a field supervisor. Though it was his regular day off, our agreement was that if one of us was off while the other was scheduled to work, picking up an overtime shift was okay. I was pleased this would be Steve's last day of work before our entire family flew to Minnesota for the weekend to attend the Vikings' first game in their new stadium.

I'd just finished dressing and was pouring my first cup of coffee when I heard the sound of footsteps outside. Tank immediately came to my side, alert and focused, until the door opened and Steve walked in, wearing the smile that always warmed my heart.

"What are you doing here?" I gave him a kiss as Tank scrambled to get some attention from Steve.

"I was in the area and I came home real quick because I just wanted to see you before you leave for work. How about we have a cup of coffee together before you head out to Palm Springs?"

WEDNESDAY, OCTOBER 5, 2016

"You got it," I said as I pulled from the cabinet his favorite ceramic mug featuring the colorful caricature image of a frog. His team members at the Lancaster Station had lovingly dubbed him "Bullfrog," and one of them had given Steve the mug as a birthday gift.

With Tank lying at my feet and Steve holding my hand across the kitchen table, a thought occurred to me. "Hon, we need to get away together; how about we plan a vacation?"

"Isn't that just what we're doing this weekend? It's going to be great having all the kids together with us at the Vikings game," he said and then sipped his coffee. "Now that they're all grown, traveling to Minnesota will be a lot easier than taking them to Disneyland, for sure."

"Steve, I've always loved our family vacations, but I want to go somewhere with *you*. Our anniversary is coming up on the twenty-third—maybe we could go on a little honeymoon together," I said with a suggestive smile.

"We'll figure it out; maybe we can do something later. Besides, we've got all the time in the world," he said with a laugh as he glanced at his watch. "I need to go, but I'll see you tonight. Be sure to text me this morning and send photos of you and Tank."

I pushed my chair away from the table, stood, and stepped into my husband's arms for one of his bear hugs I loved so much. Steve was truly my safe place. I kissed him and said, "I love you, and I'll see you tonight."

The warmth and peace that came from spending those special moments with my husband remained with me for the initial part of the drive to Palm Springs that morning, but they were soon replaced by a familiar sense of foreboding I'd first noticed several days earlier. I'd initially attributed the uneasy feeling to my long work hours and the daily round-trip drive between our home in Lancaster and my workplace at the Los Angeles sheriff's office. Oftentimes on the nightly drive home through the mountains, feeling the weariness of those long hours, I considered the possibility I could fall asleep at the wheel and be killed when my truck careened off the road. That's why, just two days earlier, I'd approached Steve and told him that I needed to talk to him.

He was stretched out on his recliner prior to going to work when I said, "Steve, I don't know what's going on with me, but I feel we need to have a conversation."

"Okay hon, tell me what's on your mind," he said as he shifted to a sitting position and gave me his full attention.

"You and I have never talked about what we'd do if something happened to one of us. What if something happened to you or me? The boys are grown and on their own, and Shannon will be soon, but what should you or I do if one of us were to die?"

A look of concern came across his face as he processed my words. "What's got you thinking about this, Tania? Is it the recent shooting?" He was, of course, referring to the July 7, 2016, sniper ambush on a group of Dallas police officers that killed five and injured nine just three months earlier. One of the officers had once worked at our station in Lancaster, which made the incident even more difficult for Steve and me, as well as the other Lancaster deputies.

"No. I don't know. Maybe. I just know that if something ever happened to me, I'd want you to know my wishes, and I'd want you to be able to move forward." I didn't tell him about my sense of uneasiness regarding my own wellbeing.

We had a productive conversation about the children, our final wishes, and our future wishes for each other should a tragedy occur. We talked about grief and the possibility of one of us being alone. We agreed that, in such an instance, after one year the remaining spouse had permission to move forward.

I felt as if the proverbial weight had been lifted from my shoulders. But then I looked at my husband and said, "Honey, come on; I know you and you can't be alone. I'm changing my mind. If you need to move forward after three months, you have my permission." Then I leaned forward, looked him in the eye, and said, "But if you bring some hooch to the house the week after I die, I promise I'll come back and haunt you!"

We both laughed; however, in reality human beings were never meant to be alone. I personally believe the single life is more difficult for men, because the Bible tells us that when God created Adam, He said, *"It is not good that man should be alone; I will make him a helper comparable to him"* (Genesis 2:18).

I continued to speak. "Steve, you belong to me, and I don't want you with anyone else, but I clearly understand that God did not mean for man to be alone. If I'm going to be gone, I give you permission to move on after three months. But I'm telling you right now that if anything ever happened to you, they'd have to take my gun away and admit me to the 2 West Mental Unit at Antelope Valley Hospital. I don't know how I'd ever survive without you."

That's when Steve laughed and said, "Oh, hon, you'd be fine. You'd have a line of dudes waiting to date you."

"I don't want a line of dudes. I only want you."

―――

By the time Tank and I arrived at the Palm Springs testing site the morning of October 5, I'd pushed aside the conversation I'd had with Steve two days earlier, along with my sense of uneasiness, to focus on the task at hand. Tank and I exited the truck and joined the other K9 teams in the secluded, desert-mountain location and its perfect topography for the extensive use of firearms planned to accustom the dogs to shooting.

As handlers we were required to engage our firearms effectively while simultaneously caring for our K9 partners. This was my first opportunity to compare Tank's skills to the others' in a simulated real-life situation. His performance quickly affirmed he was a natural at that job, and between exercises I texted Steve with updates and photos of how we were doing. He texted back each time to say how proud he was of us and what a great team Tank and I made.

As we were wrapping up morning training around 12:40, my daughter Shannon called from the parking lot of the Antelope Valley Junior College campus near our home. "Mom, I'm at school and there are a lot of police cars rolling code 3 [lights and sirens]. It must be something big because I've never seen this many police cars and unmarked cars responding to one call. What's going on?"

"Well, Shannon, I'm in Palm Springs, so I don't know. Why don't you call Dad?" I paused and then said, "No, wait; don't call him. Knowing Dad he's probably in the thick of it. I'm sure he'll let us know later."

WEDNESDAY, OCTOBER 5, 2016

Anytime Steve was in the field and I was also on duty, I made a point to listen to his radio traffic so that I knew what he was doing or if he was involved in a pursuit. But because my team was shooting that day, my radio was off. At 12:45 I checked my cell phone and saw that I'd sent the last text to him at eleven twenty, but he'd not yet responded. I thought, *Okay, he's probably busy with that code 3*, and left the matter alone as the other handlers and I prepared to go to lunch.

Tank and I climbed into my truck, but when I shifted into gear, I discovered I was stuck in the sand. With the aid of the other handlers, we got it out of the sand and then everyone drove their vehicles to a nearby burger joint. I still hadn't turned on my radio, and when I checked my phone to see if Steve had answered my text, I saw the battery was really low, so I left the phone in the truck to charge.

The dogs remained in the air-conditioned vehicles while the handlers went inside and sat at a table with our trainer. Our server had just placed large glasses of ice water in front of each of us and was handing out menus when the trainer's cell phone rang. He was seated next to me, and I couldn't help but notice his troubled expression as he listened to what the caller had to say. A moment later he turned to me and said, "Tania, it's Sergeant Wendy Zolkowski; she needs to speak to you," and then he handed me his phone.

I set aside my menu and put the phone to my ear. "Hey, Sarge, what's going on?"

"Tania, Steve's been shot. He's been rolled to the hospital."

Immediately my training kicked into action. Instead of reacting to the news, I responded with the single most important question at that moment: "Is he alive?"

"Yes, he's been taken to Antelope Valley Hospital, and we're sending a helicopter to pick you up."

I said okay and then disconnected.

I knew the AV Hospital was the best place for shooting victims in need of acute care or trauma treatment. Having accompanied numerous victims of shootings and other trauma to the hospital's emergency room, I was well acquainted with many of its doctors and nurses. Steve was exactly where he needed to be.

I told the others what had happened and then fully shifted into cop mode, compartmentalizing my emotions as I prepared to call Shannon and our sons, Chadd and Tyler.

Shannon! That's when I realized the code 3 she'd called about earlier must have involved Steve. I dialed her number, and when she answered, I said in a calm voice, "Shannon, Dad's been shot. We need to pray, and we need to get to the AV Hospital. They're sending a helicopter for me, but I don't care what you have to do—get to the hospital and go straight to Dad. Don't cry, just be strong and tell him to fight. Tell him I love him and I'm on my way."

Next I called Tyler and told him to meet his sister at the hospital, and then I called Chadd. He and his wife, Nicole, had flown out to Minnesota that morning ahead of the rest of the family to enjoy some time together before the Vikings game. Now they'd have to arrange an immediate flight back to Los Angeles.

I completed the calls to our family, including Steve's mother, Millie, and then I called our pastor so that he and our church family could pray. As I waited for the department's helicopter to pick me up, I received a call on my cell phone from Sergeant Theresa Dawson of the Lancaster Station; she was in the emergency room

WEDNESDAY, OCTOBER 5, 2016

with Steve. She told me I needed to speak to him and that she would put her phone to his ear.

I knew the words I was about to speak were important and would be defining. I remembered my initial training with the department, how it was ingrained in us that if we were ever attacked or shot in the field, we were to fight to the finish and never give up! We were trained that anytime we felt like giving up, that was the time to get mad, survive, and persevere!

This was not the time for me to cry or be weak; I needed to put on my big-girl pants and be strong for my husband. I told Steve I was on my way and to hold on; we were going to get through this together. "You need to fight! Don't give up! I need you!" I boldly declared.

But as I was talking to my husband, a thought came to me: *What if he doesn't make it? What if this is the only time I can talk to him?* I completely shifted my thinking, softening my voice. "Baby, I love you. Thank you for being an amazing husband and an incredible father. You have loved us with all of your heart. Thank you for always being there for us, no matter what. If you feel you need to go home to be with our Lord, you have my permission. I love you, and I'll be there soon—I'm on my way."

As if on cue, the moment I completed the call, the helicopter landed and Sergeant Zolkowski exited. We exchanged a hug, and then I handed her the keys to my truck so that she could drive it back to Lancaster and take Tank home.

I boarded quickly, took my seat behind the pilot and co-pilot, and quickly fastened my harness. I said hello to Lieutenant Sue Burakowski, who also had come from Los Angeles, and then put on the military-style headset that would allow me to hear radio communication between the pilot and the dispatcher.

There was no need of conversation. I remained in cop mode, in control of my emotions as we took off, my eyes fixed on my truck. For some reason, watching my vehicle appear smaller and smaller as we gained altitude caused me to recall the summer motorcycle trip Steve and I had taken only a few months ago.

We'd purchased a big red Honda Gold Wing touring bike, which we both absolutely loved. We'd often gone on camping trips with our family and other law-enforcement couples. While others traveled in their jeeps, Steve and I were always on that motorcycle.

Having been with the LASD for many years, we'd both accrued plenty of vacation time, so we'd taken an entire month to go touring with our closest friends, who were more like family. As we'd traveled throughout the country, I'd enjoyed the time in my comfortable seat behind Steve, shooting photos, reflecting on our life together, and talking to God.

I remember one day in particular as we rode through a beautiful Wyoming valley surrounded by fields of colorful wildflowers, having a very special time with God. I thanked Him for bringing Steve and me together, for our family, and for saving our marriage during a very dark time when our personal choices had nearly torn it apart. But the subsequent four years had been amazing; we were more in love than ever before. As I looked at the majestic view surrounding us, I prayed, "My God, this life and everything You've given us is so beautiful that it defies description. Lord, everything is just too perfect." And then I asked, "Is this the calm before the storm?" I didn't hear an answer.

WEDNESDAY, OCTOBER 5, 2016

But now, as the helicopter flew toward Lancaster, the memory of that question I'd asked only months ago directed my present silent prayer: *Okay, God. I now understand why You had me become Steve's wife; it was for this very moment. Whatever happens today, I'm ready. If he's paralyzed and we both have to retire, I'll be there to take care of him.*

Immediately after speaking those words to the Lord, I recalled an important conversation Steve and I had had more than once throughout our career together. We'd agreed that neither of us would want to live if we were completely immobile or in a vegetative state. Our plan was that if either of us were in that condition, at the one-month mark, if the medical opinion indicated recovery was unlikely, the other spouse would terminate medical life support, leaving the ultimate outcome in God's hands.

Looking out the window of the helicopter at the skyline, I prayed again, "God, if Steve's condition is such that he can't recover, or wouldn't want to live, then I'm asking you now to take him home."

Immediately a warm, tingling sensation began at the top of my head and moved slowly downward, as if dripping, over my face and shoulders. I felt as if I were floating. The sensation continued moving downward and then entered my heart, giving me the most amazing and tangible sense of peace. I'd never experienced anything like this peace in my life and was reminded of a verse in the Bible: *Be anxious for nothing, but in everything by prayer and supplication, with thanksgiving, let your requests be made known to God; and the peace of God, which surpasses all understanding, will guard your hearts and minds through Jesus Christ* (Philippians 4:6–7).

I turned to Lieutenant Burakowski, smiled, and told her, "We're going to be okay. God just gave me this incredible peace." She looked at me for a moment, then placed her hand on my thigh and said so kindly, "Tania, there's always hope."

I adjusted my headset in time to hear the dispatcher come over the air. "What's the ETA on the wife?" Though they'd asked this question several times during the flight, this time I felt the urgency in his words.

I was still in a state of euphoric peace as the helicopter hovered over the pad at the hospital. The parking lot and surrounding streets were filled with sheriff's vehicles, police cars, fire trucks—and *so* many people. I turned to my lieutenant and said, "As soon as we get down, you're coming with me."

I remained composed as the helicopter landed and the door opened. I removed my headset and threw it behind me. As soon as my foot hit the ground, I started running toward the ER. A sea of somber deputies had gathered at the entrance; many of their faces were familiar to me, others were not. But all eyes were on me as a man wearing a crisp white medical jacket stepped forward and gripped my arm. "Detective Owen, I'm the attending physician, and I need to talk to you," he said, his gaze steady. "Your husband was shot in the head, and a bullet is still lodged at the base of his brain."

I didn't need to hear any more. I wrestled my arm from the doctor's grasp and made my way through the silent crowd to the double doors beneath the red sign that said EMERGENCY ROOM. Though Shannon and Tyler were already in the building somewhere—hopefully together—all I wanted was to get to Steve.

WEDNESDAY, OCTOBER 5, 2016

The private room where the medical team worked on him was filled with doctors, nurses, and uniformed deputies. Steve was lying motionless on the exam table, his body shirtless and bloody. As I stepped closer, I could see his left eye had been blown out and there was a hole in his cheek. I couldn't process what I saw because in my mind he'd been shot only once. As the medical team continued to work on him, I took my husband's bloody hand and said, "Steve, you need to fight. We're going to get through this."

No sooner were the words out of my mouth than they stopped CPR. *Why are they stopping so quickly?* And then the doctor pronounced him dead at 2:44 p.m. I learned later they had given Steve over forty pints of blood and performed CPR to keep his body warm until I could arrive and hold his hand.

Only seconds after the doctor called it, I felt a disturbing tug at my leg as my team sergeant, John Hanson, removed my gun from its holster. My gun retention training triggered an initial defensive response, since we are trained to never allow anyone to take our guns. But I quickly gained control of my actions, thinking, *Why did you do that? Steve has been taken, and now you're taking my gun?* I felt terribly vulnerable, stripped of my identity and my control, yet I understood my sergeant's actions: he didn't want me to use my own gun to kill myself.

The reality of the situation hit me, and I began to cry. At that moment I wasn't Detective Tania Owen, veteran deputy sheriff who had witnessed countless tragedies and untold horrors over the years, who knew how to take control of critical situations and her emotions. I was Mrs. Steve Owen, mourning the loss of my husband. That's when I realized Shannon and Tyler were standing right behind me; they were now two young people who'd just lost their father, and I was their mother.

The three of us held each other and wept as those in the room watched in respectful silence. Then, as the silence became uncomfortable, Tyler said, "Let's pray." I'm grateful for the friend who recorded the prayer so that Tyler's words could be shared with all:

> Father, here in this moment as we carry on my father's legacy, we ask that people consider their relationship with You when they realize how fragile and short this life is. Lord, we might look at this as a hardship right now but use this tragedy for Your glory. Use this to bring people to You; use this to further Your kingdom. Lord, I pray that Your hand would be over each and every one of us now. Strengthen us with Your power, help us through this time. I pray, Lord, that You would use this to spark change—not only in this community and not only in this nation—but across the world.
>
> Lord, there is so much going on, and the biggest thing is that our nation and our world has turned against You. Let this be a reminder, Father, of the importance of You, that You should be central and the forefront of our lives. I pray Lord that the lessons my dad has taught me be carried on through each and every one of us, that we would honor him each and every day in how we act.
>
> Lord, this is only the beginning. We're going to need You; I turn it all over to You. May You be our strength, may You be our fortress, may You be our shield. Lord, each and every one of us here has been impacted in some way; let it

not stop with this room. Let us carry on the message of Your love, let us carry on the message of faith, and let us carry on the message of hope and eternal life that is only found in You. And until that day, Lord, let us continue to glorify You and further Your kingdom until we walk into those pearly gates to embrace You and embrace my dad, for we *will* see him again.

We ask all of this in Your name, and Lord, we do not doubt You but we praise You and honor You—even through this, because You have a plan for everything. And everyone said … amen.

The comfort derived from the words that remarkable young man prayed was indescribable. I knew Tyler's prayer had touched the throne of God, for the peace in that room was tangible. I felt as if I'd been wrapped in a blanket of love.

Our eldest son, Chadd, and his wife, Nicole, wouldn't arrive until after 9:00 p.m., so Steve's body, covered by an American flag, was moved to the hospital's chapel where more than fifty people—deputies, their wives, officials, and friends—gathered to honor him and offer comfort to me, Shannon, Tyler, and Steve's mother, Millie. Over and over again we heard the words, "I'm so sorry."

At that point I was emotionally numb, unable to cry. My mind reeled as I tried to process everything that had happened—was happening—all on a very public stage. The growing crowd outside the hospital now included television news trucks, their lights flooding the area as reporters sifted through the crowd in search of anyone who had known Steve and might give them a story.

When it became clear to me that Shannon, Tyler, and I were not going to be alone with Steve's body, I asked a member of the hospital staff if there was a place where my children and I could be alone together. I particularly wanted to hear Shannon's account of the day, since she had been the first to arrive at the hospital. Once we were alone, I held her hand as she shared the experience no daughter should ever have to undergo, which she now retells in her own words:

> I was in the parking lot on my college campus when I heard what sounded like gunshots coming from the neighborhood across the street. Within minutes patrol cars rolling with lights and sirens flooded the area, along with countless unmarked units.
>
> The whole scene made me nervous. My dad was working an overtime shift as a field supervisor that morning, meaning he would have been one of the first to arrive at any scene. I called his cell phone, got his voicemail, and left a message. I knew that reaching my mom was a long shot since she and Tank were testing in Palm Springs, but she took my call.
>
> When I told her what was going on and that I hadn't been able to reach Dad, she said he was probably in the middle of the situation and not to worry—he would call me back. I felt better because I knew Mom was right; Dad

WEDNESDAY, OCTOBER 5, 2016

always managed to get to the hot calls in record time, and he always called us back once the situation was under control.

I was shocked when, a short time later, Mom called back and said Dad had been shot. She didn't yet know his condition, but told me to go directly to Antelope Valley Hospital; the department had arranged for a helicopter to get her there as soon as possible.

Pulling into a space in the hospital parking lot, I slammed my gearshift into park, grabbed my purse, and ran through the entrance doors to the emergency room. Once inside, I called out "Dad?" to a large group of deputies gathered in the waiting area, expecting him to answer me. The only response was the look of horror on the deputies' faces when they turned and saw me standing there.

Several deputies who knew our family came quickly to my side and, along with a few nurses, escorted me to a back room to wait for information from the doctors. The deputies bombarded me with questions: "Where are your brothers? How far away are they? What do we need to do to get them and the rest of your family here?"

After what seemed a lifetime, the doctor came in and proceeded to give me more information than I could process. The only sentence I heard was, "Your dad has been shot in the face." *Okay, people survive being shot in the face,* I told myself. *This isn't the end game.*

The doctor excused himself to perform another scan. When he returned a short time later, he asked if I'd like to come be with my dad. Without hesitation I said yes; I needed to see Dad for myself and tell him everything would be okay, that Mom and the rest of the family would be here soon.

The moment I walked into the room where they were working on him, I thought they'd made a mistake. The man on the table couldn't be my dad. *My* dad has been shot only once in the face; this man's face had multiple wounds. Tissue and blood oozed from his temple, cheeks, and mouth where the bullets had entered, causing severe bruising that made his face unrecognizable.

But as I looked at his arm, the unmistakable tattoo heart bearing my mom's name confirmed what I already knew but couldn't bring myself to believe. His bare chest had a dark bruise in the area over his heart where, a deputy explained, Dad's badge had deflected one of the shots.

Someone provided a chair so that I could sit and hold his hand while the medical team worked on him. I couldn't believe how cold his hand felt; the only warmth came from the constant flow of blood they administered to him, much of which ran down his arm and onto our hands.

While several nurses alternately performed CPR, I rested my head on Dad's hand as my body chemistry normalized following the adrenaline rush it had just experienced. That's when I accepted what I knew was to come.

The voices in the room became nothing more than white noise as a machine suctioned the blood from Dad's mouth to clear his airway. With each CPR compression I could literally hear the stress on his ribs. At one point they got Dad's pulse back for a few seconds, but it never returned.

WEDNESDAY, OCTOBER 5, 2016

Once Mom arrived, they called it; the medical team had kept him "alive" until she got there. When I looked down at the blood that covered my hands and puddled at my feet, causing my shoes to stick to the floor, I felt as if I were living in a nightmare.

Shannon was right—we *were* living in a nightmare—but we had no choice other than to move forward.

Our eldest son, Chadd, and his wife, Nicole, arrived around 10:00 p.m. and we spent some time together in the room with Steve and the dozens of deputies and sheriff's department personnel who had chosen to remain there. When it was time for the procession to the Los Angeles County Coroner's Office to begin, the blood-stained American flag that had covered my husband for the past eight hours was removed, folded, and handed to me. His body was wrapped and moved into the waiting hearse. I rode with another officer in a sheriff's vehicle directly behind the hearse while Chadd, Nicole, Tyler, Millie, and Shannon followed in a vehicle behind us.

As the procession pulled out of the hospital parking lot at 11:00 p.m., I was stunned to see the number of people still gathered in every direction. Not just law enforcement officers and other first responders, but also the citizens of the community we served. The freeway and flag-draped overpasses were lined with people, young and old of every race, all of them waving and saluting as the procession passed by. "My God, how long have they been waiting?" I said to no one in particular.

An hour and a half later, we exited onto Mission Road in Los Angeles, where the streets were packed with officers who kept every intersection open for us. When we pulled into the driveway at the coroner's office, the entire bomb squad unit I served with was there in uniform, standing at attention and saluting. I was so thankful to those men and women, who are family to me, for honoring my husband and making me feel so loved.

Once Steve's body was moved inside, Homicide Detectives Karen Shonka and Wayne Holston pulled me aside. That's when I learned what had happened: Steve had answered a burglary-in-progress call and had been the first to arrive. The suspect had initially shot him once in the head and then stood over his body and unloaded the rest of the rounds in his gun.

Chapter Two

A VERY PUBLIC GOODBYE

Tania Owen

By the next morning flags in California had been lowered to half-staff, and local television stations had suspended regular programming for ongoing news coverage about the murder of Sergeant Steve Owen.

Oftentimes we hear reports of deputies or officers killed in the line of duty, which happens in different ways: being struck by a vehicle while directing traffic or a traffic collision while responding to an emergency, for instance. Steve had not been killed in the line of duty—he had been murdered. Los Angeles County Sheriff Jim McDonnell honored Steve and announced the details surrounding his death in this televised public statement from the Lancaster Sheriff's Station:

> Today we mourn the loss of a man who made a difference to his family, his fellow deputies, and his community. I want to thank the reporters who have taken the time to describe the numerous acts of kindness, service, and mentoring that define the life of Sergeant Steve Owen. Thank you to those who have placed flowers and candles at this memorial, who took the time to tell his colleagues how much he will be missed. Thank you to the men, women, and children who are describing in great detail the inspired conversations they had with Sergeant Owen. They are saying that on their worst day, he made them believe that tomorrow would be a better one.
>
> Today I was able to spend time with his family, and they are devastated, as you can imagine. I've been with our deputies, many who knew Steve Owen for decades. Some have only known him for a while, but long enough to know how much he had to teach, and how much they, as young deputies, had to learn. This is a reminder that our relationship with you, our public, is not political; it's personal.
>
> The political discourse nationally and here in California about criminal justice reform, the broad-brush criticism of officers' tactics, and important conversation about inherent bias in law enforcement are important and necessary conversations we are having. However, today I ask that we lower our voices and raise our sights to see that in the life

and death of Sergeant Steve Owen it came down to this: a life of service to others, a 911 call for help, a predator armed with a gun, and a deputy sworn to protect his community doing all he could to stand between danger and the rest of the public that we are privileged to serve.

Sergeant Steve Owen lost his life in that very profound moment but will remain with us for a lifetime. It's our tradition to reserve the term *hero* only for those recognized for acts of heroism. It's a word intentionally reserved for Sergeant Steve Owen. We will speak of Steve Owen for the deputy he was, a man who by all accounts exemplified all that we stand for at the Los Angeles County Sheriff's Department. He is, and always will be, an important part of our history and American history as well, a man worth remembering.

The suspect—I won't mention his name here—first came into our custody as a juvenile, selling marijuana as many others do. He then graduated to more serious crimes, where he was arrested eleven times, two of which resulted in state prison terms. He will fade away in the judicial process that will ultimately adjudicate his case. If convicted, he will face yet more time in prison, and—this is what I want our public to understand—if the trend of legislative mandates continues, he may get another opportunity to return to our community for yet another attempt at rehabilitation and redemption—and possibly another chance for another murder.

Here was a guy, a parolee classified as a moderate risk. We see that these risk assessments have their limitations.

Yesterday he was a parolee walking on our streets with a stolen gun; today he is facing charges of murdering a peace officer.

Sergeant Owen approached the suspect in response to a burglary call. The suspect immediately shot Sergeant Owen. He then stood over him and executed Sergeant Owen by firing four additional rounds into his body. Next, he unsuccessfully searched the body for the sergeant's weapon, with the intent to murder the first responding deputy.

The responding deputy engaged the suspect, who had pointed his weapon at him. The responding deputy fired numerous times, striking the suspect once in the shoulder. Not only did the suspect want to kill our deputies, he held two teenagers hostage in a house until they were rescued by the heroic efforts of our Special Enforcement Bureau and our Lancaster Station personnel. He was subsequently arrested in a surrounding neighborhood without further incident.

Once again I want to thank you for being with us today and for respecting the privacy of the Owen family.

Lancaster is the northernmost city in Los Angeles County, a high-desert community often described as a melting pot of demographics. On Thursday and Friday it seemed as though the entire community had shut down to follow the continual television news reports. Interestingly, a number of former criminals came forward to talk to the media about Steve and to tell their stories about how his intervention and influence had changed the course of their lives. The news coverage was constant. Reporters hounded anyone in uniform in an effort to get an interview with me, but deputies protected our family as best they could from the ongoing media circus.

During the day our family gathered in my home while we took care of the immediate business at hand. Sheriff's department personnel were there with documents to be signed regarding benefits and retirement, and to set in motion plans for Steve's funeral the following week, now expected to draw national attention. I was thankful that our pastors, John Santero—also a first responder—and Jason Grundy of The Road Church of the Antelope Valley, were also there to support us and pray for us in the midst of our very public loss.

I was bone tired from the nonstop traffic in my home Thursday, so I was happy to excuse myself late in the day to go feed our horses and the other animals that populated our small ranch. Tank was at my side when Max, Steve's big, black Percheron gelding, came up behind me and nuzzled my back, gently nickering as if to ask where Steve was. I turned and stroked the white blaze on his forehead as I looked into his kind, dark eyes. "I'm so sorry, Max, but he's not coming home," I said, unable to stop the tears that streamed down my face.

Steve and Max had for years been part of the Los Angeles County Mounted Enforcement Detail that assisted with crowd management, wildfire livestock evacuation, patrol, and ceremonial events. They had undergone intense training together, after which Max earned his own deputy's badge that he wore on his regulation breast collar while on duty. Closing the chapter of Steve's and Max's service together was yet another aspect of this unimagined loss.

The busyness and grief that permeated Thursday and Friday were unrelenting, yet the sense of peace I'd first experienced on the helicopter flight on Wednesday remained with me. That's why, when Chadd came up with an idea to get our family away from the media circus going on in our county, I said yes.

Though Chadd had donated our football game tickets to another family, he and Tyler decided they wanted the Vikings organization to know what had happened to their father. Their idea was to honor not only Steve—but all the law enforcement deputies and officers who had lost their lives in 2016—on the Jumbotron during the game. Following Chadd's call to the organization, not only did the Vikings agree to honor Steve and the others as requested, they also provided our entire family, including Steve's mother, VIP tickets to the game. And through the generosity and assistance of both Lancaster and Minneapolis law enforcement, our flights were rescheduled, and the cost was covered.

I had absolute peace about our decision to attend the game. I wanted to honor my husband, and this was a tangible way to do so. Besides, had we not gone, Steve would without a doubt have said, "You're a bunch of retards—I would have gone!"

I smiled as our flight took off from LAX, my eyes fixed on the bag stowed beneath the seat in front of mine. In it was the carefully folded, blood-stained American flag that had been draped over my husband's body, which now accompanied us on this mission to honor him on a national stage.

On the day of the big game we were given sideline passes so that we could meet members of the Vikings football team staff. We made it a point to meet every member of the Minneapolis Police Department working the game that day, all of whom stood at attention during the moment of silence held in honor of Steve and the other members of law enforcement just prior to kickoff. That televised moment drew a standing ovation in the stadium.

The love shown for Steve and the other members of law enforcement gave us the ability to relax and truly enjoy the game. As we sat together as a family, we often commented that Dad had the best seat in the house.

The Vikings won their game against the Texans that day, and we were presented with one of the game balls. After the teams went to their locker rooms and the crowd began to clear, Chadd and Tyler stepped onto the field and tossed the football back and forth as the rest of us watched. Steve's mother, Millie, looked at me and said, "Tania, this is like a piece of heaven on earth."

The time spent in Minneapolis had indeed been the respite our family needed, but the following day we were on a flight back to Los Angeles—and reality. Though that reality included finalizing plans for Steve's funeral, I'd also made an important decision about how I would move forward with my life.

Steve and I had both been Christians when we'd married and become a blended family that included his two young boys and my daughter. As a family we were strong in our faith; however, the culture of law enforcement at that time respected one's religion as a private matter. Neither Steve nor I hid our faith while at work;

rather, we held our relationship with Christ "close to the vest," as the saying goes.

Our marriage had had its ups and downs for sure, the downs being particularly devastating. Law enforcement marriages experience a heightened amount of stress on spouses and families, and we were no exception. But Steve and I also had known that no matter how intense the pressure or destructive the behavior, God was faithful to anyone who would turn to Him and allow Him to heal that which was seemingly broken beyond repair. Steve and I had recently made the decision to proactively share our faith with younger law enforcement couples and marriages so that they could avoid many of the pitfalls we'd experienced. Sadly, we never had the chance to take this hands-on approach.

Now, as I continued to experience the supernatural sense of peace that had remained with me since the day of Steve's murder, I decided to make a point in telling the world how much I love God and about the relationship Steve and I had had together with Christ at its center. My prayer as we planned the funeral was, "Lord, if we can bring just one soul to you during Steve's service, I know both You and he will be well pleased."

But I didn't have to wait until the funeral to tell others about Steve's and my relationship with God.

Early the following week I was invited to attend the debriefing at the Lancaster Station concerning Steve's murder. At a debriefing, our homicide detectives handling the case would gather with station personnel in a conference room. The detectives would break down what occurred and provide the information they had gathered so far, supported by video and recordings of the radio traffic. That day was no exception.

Our entire family was invited to attend, and though I was not working, because of the pride I felt for my profession, I chose to wear my uniform, accompanied by Tank in his K9 vest. I also wanted to make the point that the murderer was not going to take two of us out. Nothing was going to keep me from fulfilling the oath I made to serve, and Steve would have expected nothing less from his wife. At the end of the meeting, the lieutenant in charge looked at me and said, "Tania, would you like to say a few words?"

"No. I'm just here for the debriefing," I said. But then I realized this was a good opportunity for me to thank everyone for all they had done, and were doing, for me and for our family. As I stood and faced the dozens of my fellow deputies in the room, the weight of grief was apparent on their faces. I also sensed the presence of a dangerous mindset hovering in the room: a mindset of *what if?*

Many of the deputies in that room had been in the field the day Steve was murdered, and I'm sure they'd all asked themselves questions such as, "What if I'd arrived a few seconds earlier?" "What if I'd taken a different route to the call?" "What if Steve hadn't come to work on his day off?"

I knew I had to put a stop to all the what ifs.

Still experiencing the ever-present sense of peace that had surrounded me now for days, I took a deep breath and said, "Listen, guys. We can talk about the what ifs all day long, but all that's going to do is feed our grief. What if I'd been there ten seconds earlier? What if the sky was purple? What if the sun was square? Don't do it!

Let me tell you something: it doesn't matter what any of you might have done; my husband was going home to God that day."

For nearly an hour I talked about who Steve was as a husband and father. I talked about our marriage, our life together, and our love for God. I even told them about the conversation we'd had two days before he died in which we'd given each other permission to move forward, and my telling Steve I knew he couldn't wait a year. Then I related my threat to come back and haunt him if he brought another woman into our house.

Telling that story broke the heaviness. So I continued, now walking around the room: "If any of you are experiencing pain right now or you are dealing with anger, it's time to give it to God and trust Him to replace it with the same peace He's given me. I can tell you this peace is real. How else can anyone explain my being here today and speaking these words of truth like this?"

I concluded by inviting everyone there to join me at The Road Church the following Sunday. Many came up to me afterward to tell me how much they'd been affected by my words and to let me know they'd be at church on Sunday.

The morning of October 13, 2016, was ushered in with clear skies and comfortable temperatures. I was thankful for a beautiful day as I did what I knew thousands of other men and women in law enforcement were doing at this very moment: stepping into our dress uniforms in preparation for the funeral of Sergeant Steve Owen.

The service would be held at the Lancaster Baptist Church, which could accommodate a large group in both its spacious sanctuary and its overflow facility where the service would be streamed. Before our procession arrived, thousands of men and women in uniform already lined the sidewalks of the multi-facility campus as they awaited the arrival of the hearse bearing my husband's body. Several hundred deputies on motorcycles led the motorcade, two-by-two, red and blue lights flashing, followed by LASD escort vehicles. Our family rode directly behind the hearse in several black limousines.

Upon turning into the campus, the vehicle escorts pulled into their designated area as the hearse came to a stop. I exited the limousine and, escorted by a fellow deputy, walked behind the hearse as it moved slowly forward to the entrance of the church.

A few feet behind me, Deputy Hil Goedhart led Steve's black horse, Max, followed by members of the Los Angeles County Mounted Enforcement Detail. The tradition of a riderless horse during funeral processions and military parades dates back to ancient Rome and symbolizes fallen soldiers. In accordance with tradition, Steve's boots were inserted backwards in the stirrups as a symbol of his looking back toward the living one last time before riding into eternity.

Inside the sanctuary, as music played and people streamed in, filling the sanctuary and balcony, a huge screen displayed photo and video images of Steve with his family and serving with the LASD. On the stage behind the pulpit, hundreds of uniformed deputies were seated in the choir loft. Some in attendance had traveled hundreds of miles to be there; a few had traveled across the country more than a thousand miles.

Pastor Paul Chappell stepped to the pulpit and welcomed our family, friends, members of law enforcement, and the many dignitaries in attendance. The first to speak were local and state government representatives, followed by members of the Los Angeles County Sheriff's Department. Steve's fellow deputies described him as being a bigger-than-life sergeant who fed the hungry and comforted the traumatized while making sure the bad guys went to jail. They talked of his commitment to service, to his family, and to God.

Perhaps the most touching moment came when Detective Mitch Speed sang the first of the three songs we'd selected for the service. Standing next to the large poster of a smiling Steve mounted on Max, Mitch delivered a powerful rendition of "American Lawman" as video images of Steve moved across the screen.

Chadd, Tyler, and Shannon each spoke about their father, and Steve's mother, Millie, reminded everyone how Jesus' mother, Mary, must have felt as she watched her son endure a brutal death, a literal execution on the cross, to pay the price for mankind's sin, once and for all.

At my request, Chadd read the letter I'd composed for everyone in attendance to tell them about Steve Owen, the father and husband:

> Twenty years ago I met the love of my life. I feel so blessed to have been known as Mrs. Steve Owen. Most everyone here knows Steve as Sergeant Owen. I want to tell you about Steve Owen, my husband.
>
> Steve was the love of my life. He was tender. He was sweet. He was kind, and he was a humble man. Most importantly, he was a godly man. He made me feel like the most special girl in the world.

On our days off he would make me coffee, and on Sundays he would bring me breakfast in bed. We would sit together, and he would read the Bible to me. He was my big teddy bear and my protector; I always felt safe with him.

A lot of people don't know that Steve loved to garden. He planted a variety of trees including apple, nectarine, peach, plumb, apricot, and cherry. He also planted peppers, garlic, tomatoes, onions, and cilantro—everything needed to make salsa. The way he grew his garden is the way he nurtured me, and our love continued to grow.

We blended our families and raised three beautiful children. As you can imagine, raising a blended family is not always easy, but we persevered because of his amazing love and leadership for our family.

I experienced a great life with Steve. As a family we went camping every year. He wanted to make sure each trip was a learning experience for the kids and me. We visited many national parks and lakes. Our most favorite lake is Lake Powell, in northern Arizona. Steve taught us all how to water ski. He was a great water skier, and I loved looking at his muscles as he skied. I wasn't as good as Steve. As a matter of fact, I didn't even come close, but he never gave up on me. He was my biggest cheerleader.

Trying to describe the love I feel for Steve is like trying to count the stars. It would be endless, and I would always try to find more.

Steve, you are my best friend, my safe place, my calm waters, and even, sometimes, my rough seas. I love you to the deepest amount of my soul. You have my heart for always, until I see you again in heaven, my love.

The room was silent as Chadd finished reading my letter and set it aside. Then he spoke directly to all in attendance.

> The stories we've heard throughout this past week have put us in absolute awe of our father. He never talked to us about the people whose lives he touched and changed forever through his grace, love, and giving heart. He saved numerous people and encouraged them, not only with brutal honesty, but by providing them with shoes, a meal, clothes, and most importantly, a direction to go with their lives—a landmark called the cross.
>
> The pursuits and exciting career moments were great, but the stories about the lives he touched were much more important. My dad didn't speak about these stories; they were just a part of how he lived his life each and every day. He was the epitome of humility.
>
> I do know this: our dad isn't going anywhere. He is in heaven right now, watching over this community and us. He is with Jesus, his Lord and Savior, my Lord and Savior, our Lord and Savior. In closing I want to leave you with this challenge: Press in to the Lord during this trying time; He is your rock, your shelter, your comforter. Only He can provide you with the peace that surpasses all understanding.

Though the funeral procession and service had been planned according to protocol and implemented to this point with military precision, the Owen family was unwavering in our conviction that everyone in attendance be given the opportunity to know Jesus as their Lord and Savior too.

Pastor Paul Chappell again stepped to the podium and announced that the peace so apparent on the Owen family was available to everyone seated in the church, the overflow auditorium, and those watching the televised broadcast at home. He talked of God's forgiveness and the decision Steve had once made to receive Jesus as his Lord and Savior. Pastor Chappell then led everyone in a prayer of salvation. Many of those in the sanctuary immediately acknowledged their decisions for Christ, and we learned later that even more who'd watched remotely had also received Jesus.

As I stood to take my place next to Steve's American flag-draped coffin, I knew how pleased he would be to see that many lives had been changed that day, just as his had once been changed when he came to Christ.

With peace in my heart, I proudly gave my husband the traditional, slow military salute and then escorted his casket from the sanctuary as a lone, kilt-clad piper played "Amazing Grace."

Chapter Three

MARCH 2016

Vickie Speed

Each spring law enforcement officers from around the globe converge on Baker, California, to compete in the Baker to Vegas Challenge Cup Relay in hopes of winning the coveted cup trophy. Over the past thirty-plus years, literally hundreds of thousands have participated in the 120-mile run across the desert to Las Vegas, often described as "the largest and most prestigious law enforcement foot pursuit in the world."

My fifty-year-old husband, Mitch, had been part of the Lancaster Station Sheriff's Department team since joining the Los Angeles County Sheriff's Department in 2002. Having been a runner his whole life, Mitch particularly looked forward to the annual event—even more so as the 2016 race approached. This would be the first year I didn't go with him; instead, our son, Brodie, planned to come home from college that weekend to attend in my place. When Brodie first presented the idea of just the two of them going together, my initial thought was, *What an incredible father-son weekend this will be.*

I was so pleased that Brodie and his dad would experience this inspiring race weekend designed to promote the ideals of teamwork, camaraderie, physical fitness, and competition. The event had grown so much over the past thirty years that the number of teams were now limited to three hundred, running in hourly flights between Saturday at 8:00 a.m. through Sunday evening. The race included divisions for men, women, and co-ed teams. The highlight of the weekend was the Sunday awards ceremony at the Hilton Hotel and Convention Center, attended by some eight thousand people consisting of runners and their families, race personnel, and volunteers.

As always Mitch had begun his training the previous fall with runs that varied from seven to ten miles each. Having started his running career in high school, he was accustomed to giving 100 percent to his training, always pushing to better his time with each subsequent year. But this year had been different. His time had actually been slower than the previous year, and he'd struggled with the runs. As a result, he hadn't trained as frequently as in previous years.

Mitch was a little upset with his time and grudgingly admitted that perhaps his age was affecting his performance. I knew my husband well enough to know his nature was to take mental control of a challenging situation and work through it, yet it seemed he was taking a less than aggressive approach to his training than usual.

When it came time to choose which portion of the race to run, he selected the shorter 5.5-mile leg on mostly flat terrain.

The weather was absolutely beautiful the morning of the race, and Brodie kept me posted throughout the day on Lancaster Station's progress. My son was there rooting for his dad and giving him pep talks. Mitch typically ran a 6.5-minute mile; needless to say, he was really disappointed to learn he'd run a 7.5-minute mile that day. Brodie teased Mitch, saying, "Dad, you're an old man, and you didn't train like you should have during the winter: your poor time is your own fault!" They had a good laugh over Mitch's performance and then went and enjoyed a five-star steak dinner after the awards ceremony. Both told me it was one of the best dinners and conversations they'd ever had, and I was so grateful for the time they'd spent together that special weekend.

Once Mitch was back at home and we had a chance to talk about the race, he told me how disappointed he was with his performance. "Vic, it was really weird. About a half mile from the finish line, I literally wanted to lie down and die. I've been a runner since high school, and I've never had anything like that happen before."

"You'll get 'em next year," I said with a laugh. "After all, you didn't really train this year the way you've done in the past."

A few weeks later as we were having dinner one evening, Mitch informed me that he was having some "man problems." When I asked what he meant, he said, "It's nothing to worry about. The guys at the station and I have been Googling my symptoms, and we've got it figured out."

Seems I was having my own man problem with communication at the moment, so I persisted with questions until he told me that the problem had to do with urination. "Mitch, I know this is a common issue with men your age, but you really should consider going to a doctor and getting it checked out," I said. He told me he wasn't ready to do that, so I said okay and let the matter go.

Then the first week in May, Mitch made a surprise visit to my office, where I worked as a project manager for a construction company. Though he occasionally stopped by to say hi when he was on duty in the area, the moment he shut my office door and took a seat, I knew this was a serious visit.

When our eyes locked, it was as if I were seeing him through a different lens: his skin appeared jaundiced and his eyes a little gray. I spoke first, saying, "Honey, what's going on?"

"I have to talk to you, Vic—I don't feel well."

"So, when you say you don't feel well, what do you mean?"

"I think you know I haven't felt well for a while, but I'm telling you I *really* don't feel well."

Instead of suggesting he see a doctor, I said, "Okay, Mitch, what do you want me to do?"

He asked me to contact Stephanie, our physician's assistant and a dear family friend, and ask if he could come see her immediately. I texted her and learned it was her day off, but after updating her on Mitch's symptoms over the past couple of months, she asked that I take him directly to our nearby Urgent Care to get started on lab work and then she would see us the following day. We did as she asked and then went home so that Mitch could rest.

We arrived fifteen minutes early at our doctor's office the next day, but Mitch and I didn't wait long in the exam room before Stephanie came in, lab work in hand. The look of concern on her face spoke volumes. Though I was surprised when Mitch asked if I would step out of the room so that he could talk to her privately, I complied. When I was invited back in a short time later, I said, "What's going on?" Mitch didn't respond; instead, Stephanie looked me straight in the eye and said, "Vickie, we need to get Mitch into the City of Hope right away. He needs to see a urologic oncologist."

In other words, *Mitch has cancer.*

Stephanie stepped out of the room to make the phone call, and when I looked at Mitch, he appeared neither shocked nor concerned. That's when I decided I'd wait until we got home to talk to him about the matter. I instinctively reached out and took his hand—the familiar gesture that had always assured me everything would be all right. We sat in silence until Stephanie returned and told us Mitch had an appointment with a City of Hope urologist, Dr. Donald Hannoun, the following Thursday. We thanked her, she hugged each of us, and then we left the exam room.

I was still holding Mitch's hand as we exited the building and walked in silence toward our vehicle. We'd taken about ten steps when Mitch stopped, turned to me, and said, "Look at me." So, I did.

"Vickie, we will not ask *why?* We will never say, 'Why us?' We will always say, 'Why not us?' And we will ask God to use us. Do I make myself clear? Do you hear me?"

I honestly didn't understand what had just happened at the doctor's office, but I knew from his firm tone Mitch was serious, so I said, "Yes, Mitch, I hear you." Half an hour later, in the familiar comfort of our home, he and I had a discussion that set the course of our immediate future.

"Mitch, you need to tell me what's *really* going on here," I said.

"I believe you know. We're going to the City of Hope, but I think it's important at this point not to get ahead of ourselves. Let's just wait and see what the results are following next week's visit."

Though no one had yet actually said the word *cancer*, we knew. The City of Hope was, after all, one of the nation's leading comprehensive cancer centers. Looking back at the past year—his difficulty in training for the race, his feeling that he wanted to die as he ran the Baker to Vegas, his not feeling well—I realized Mitch had known he was sick for some time, yet he'd chosen, as always, to protect his family. That was the moment things shifted for me.

The first thought that came to my mind was a phrase from our marriage vows: *in sickness and in health, in the good times and in the bad*. Of course, when we took those vows there wasn't yet much depth to them because we were young and hadn't really lived. We'd never faced serious illness, and for the most part we'd known only good times in our marriage, though we'd had our share of rough patches. God had always been faithful to see us through every challenge we faced, and I knew He was with us now.

The possibility of facing cancer with Mitch was a battle I wasn't prepared for, but I knew that with God I was strong. Mitch had told me one of the reasons he married me was that I was so strong, that if something ever happened to him, he knew I would take care of our family and be able to go on with my life. Now it was time for me to stand by my husband's side, to be his strength. I knew I would do whatever I had to do to care for him and protect him—just as he had always protected our family.

We met with Dr. Hannoun at the City of Hope the following Thursday and instantly liked him. His experience and expertise gave us comfort as he explained the first step was to get a biopsy so that we'd know exactly what we were dealing with. After taking twelve tissue biopsies of Mitch's prostate that day, Dr. Hannoun said, "Okay, Mitch and Vickie, as soon as we get the results, I'll call you. Then based on the facts, we'll set up an appropriate treatment plan. In the meantime, go home and have a great Memorial Day weekend together."

We were at home that Saturday entertaining some friends when Mitch's cell phone rang. It was Dr. Hannoun. We excused ourselves and stepped into our home office to put the doctor on speaker for the news that would change our lives: "Mitch, all twelve tissue samples tested positive. You have a very aggressive stage-4 prostate cancer, and we need to get you in here immediately to come up with a plan."

I don't recall the rest of the lengthy conversation—I was trying to wrap my mind around "stage 4." I'm certainly not a medical expert; however, having witnessed my dad's battle with cancer a number of years earlier, I understood that stage-4 cancer was *metastatic*, meaning it had spread from its origin to other parts of the body.

Following the call with Dr. Hannoun, Mitch and I sat there looking at each other. We didn't cry, and we didn't speak for a few minutes. It occurred to me that what the doctor had just said hadn't taken my husband by surprise. Mitch was obviously giving me time to process what we'd heard. When we did speak, we agreed we would face this "thing" head on, and we would face it together. We needed to tell our son and the rest of the family, but we decided to wait until the following day. In the meantime we had company to attend to.

Mitch's mother, Barbara Speed, was a firm believer in the saying "When life gives you lemons, make lemonade." She'd raised Mitch to always look for good, even in a bad situation, and then to approach that situation with faith, for the Bible says, *And we know that all things work together for good to those who love God, to those who are called according to his purpose* (Roman 8:28). That is exactly how Mitch viewed his upcoming battle with cancer.

No one wants to hear the word *cancer*. When a friend or loved one says, "I have cancer," people typically react with a startled gasp, followed by a look of pity. Mitch didn't want others to feel sorry for him, and he certainly didn't want them to be sad.

"Vic, I know the world sees cancer as darkness, but I want to show them the light in the midst of that darkness. I want everyone to see the positive that can come from this."

I said, "Mitch, I know you can do anything you set your mind to, so what's your plan?"

He picked up his Bible. "Last night I opened my Bible and read this verse: *A man's heart plans his way, but the Lord directs his steps* (Proverbs 16:9). I've asked God to show me how to be a light to the world, how I can wake up each day and change the world in the time I have left. I don't have a plan yet, but I believe God will show me exactly what to do."

Oh, how I loved that man!

Our son, Brodie, came home from school the following week so that he could go with us to meet with Dr. Hannoun about Mitch's treatment plan. As the three of us took our seats with the doctor the day of the meeting, the depth of the love I felt for my husband and son kicked me into mama-bear mode. I felt supernatural strength rise up in me, and I knew I would do anything and everything I could to protect and comfort Mitch and Brodie in the coming days, weeks, months—however long we were in this battle.

The meeting was difficult because the facts were hard to hear. Mitch remained stoic, but Brodie was understandably upset; it was a lot to take in for a young man who so loved his father, the man who'd always been Brodie's hero. Dr. Hannoun explained the best initial course of action was chemotherapy, beginning in July and ending in October. We asked a lot of questions, which Dr. Hannoun patiently answered, and then Mitch asked the one question that had been suspended like an ominous cloud in the room: "So, doctor, based on the facts as we know them, what's my expected longevity?"

Dr. Hanoun paused, directing his answer to Mitch. "Of course, no two cases are the same; however, 50 percent of stage-4 patients like you live five to ten years."

Mitch responded with a slight nod of his head and then leaned forward and said, "Well, if the experts say five to ten, then we might as well plan on fifteen to twenty—because this cancer doesn't know who it's dealing with!" With that statement, my husband had just raised the Speed-family battle flag.

Chemotherapy would not begin for a couple of weeks yet, so after dinner that evening we had a family meeting to address the next set of issues that required decisions.

Mitch would notify the sheriff's department about his diagnosis and the upcoming treatment plan. In addition to vacation time, he also had plenty of sick leave, which ensured he would be paid while undergoing chemo. For once I was thankful to be married to a man who seldom took vacations.

I also would need to adjust my work schedule. The construction company I'd worked for the past ten years was family owned, and I knew they would be open to my working a flexible schedule as needed so that I could help Mitch.

Next was Brodie. He lived on campus at the college he attended about eighty miles from our home. Since his current classes were all on the same two days each week, he proposed moving home and commuting. Mitch and I agreed. But what we didn't agree to was Brodie delaying his planned entry to graduate school. He'd already been accepted to the University of San Francisco's master's program, and I was glad when Mitch said, "You're going. Period." With that, the matter was settled, and we were ready to move forward as a family with Mitch's upcoming chemotherapy.

Or so we thought.

Without warning, Mitch went into kidney failure, which required the placement of a nephrostomy tube, a catheter inserted through the skin into the kidney to drain urine and calm the kidneys. Then, just when we thought he was stable, he developed a horrible infection and was hospitalized. Thankfully, his medical team was well prepared to deal with the issue, and they released him within a week's time.

But by the time he got home much had already changed. As part of his treatment plan Mitch received an injection intended to reduce his body's levels of male hormones to stop them from fueling prostate cancer cells. I remember him looking at me and saying,

"Do you know what this means, Vickie?" When I said no, he went on to explain that we'd never have sexual relations again.

I was stunned. Mitch and I had always enjoyed our physical intimacy and I certainly was not ready to give up that aspect of our relationship. But I had no choice in the matter—having sex with my husband just ended. Surprisingly to me, it didn't matter. All I cared about was Mitch beating cancer.

Mitch's chemo treatments started in July as scheduled, and if someone hadn't already known he had cancer, they'd never have suspected. He didn't feel sick, and he looked great. I was confident the treatments were going stop the cancer. My husband was a strong man, his well-known mantra being "Speed Strong." I knew if anybody could beat this kind of cancer, it was Mitch.

But I wanted to do my part too. I wanted to be sure he was eating a healthy diet, so I spent hours online researching cancer, the best foods to eat, and what not to eat. I purged our kitchen of all processed food, purchased a juicer, and planned every meal with the precision of a culinary samurai. I was determined to give Mitch every opportunity to beat this thing.

Although I had known we'd have the support of the men and women of the Lancaster Station who'd been like family to Mitch for many years, I had not expected the level of support shown my husband from the City of Lancaster. Mitch was a singer, and as such he'd performed the national anthem at the Fourth of July celebration, rodeos, and just about every City of Lancaster event in recent years. Mitch's relationship with the city wasn't merely a working relationship; it was a precious friendship.

For this reason he was greatly honored to receive an invitation to come to the city hall in August, where he would be given the key to the city. At first, uneasy with the attention, he didn't want to go, but with a little encouragement he finally accepted the invitation. When we arrived at the Lancaster City Hall that Tuesday night, most of our family members were already there, along with about one hundred law-enforcement men and women in uniform. At the head of the room were the mayor, vice-mayor, and members of the city council, who each commended Mitch for his representation of the City of Lancaster. They thanked him for his faithfulness and principled service, and in turn, he thanked them for standing with us as we faced the journey ahead.

Though Mitch felt well and had no adverse reactions to chemotherapy, it bothered me to see the looks of concern on the faces of the members of his department who surrounded him that night. I assumed it was because they'd heard about his early-on kidney failure, but as Mitch and I left the building together he said, "Vic, did you notice how everyone was looking at me?"

"Well, yeah—you just got the key to the city."

"No, that's not it. They think I'm dying."

"What?" I was stunned to hear him say such a thing.

"It's that special diet you've got me on. I'm so skinny, they all think I'm dying!"

Needless to say, I put the control of Mitch's diet back in his hands—though I was happy he hadn't lost his sense of humor.

Near the end of September Mitch got a call from one of his fellow deputies. The deputy told Mitch his friends at the Lancaster Station were hosting a luau at the University of Antelope Valley ballroom on Saturday the twenty-sixth and that Mitch and I were to be there—no questions asked.

Of course, we assumed they'd planned something nice for Mitch, but we were totally unprepared for what we saw when we stepped into the ballroom that night. The room was wall-to-wall with people—deputies in both uniform and civilian clothing, representatives of the business community, the city council, and so many friends and family—who gave us a standing ovation upon our entrance. Mitch and I were so moved that we cried.

I remember thinking, *Oh my gosh, this is for us. They love my husband so much.* It took a while to grasp everything going on: the DJ, the food, the open bar, and the highlight of the fundraiser evening, a live auction.

Mitch and I were escorted to the head table, where a constant stream of well-wishers stopped by to express their love and support. One of the gifts he received that evening was a pair of boxing gloves that signified the fight he was in, on which were written messages of support and love from his friends. I'd never seen my husband happier than he was that night, surrounded by hundreds of people, all of whom we considered family.

An hour or so later, my heart was full as I watched Mitch move through the crowd, methodically acknowledging each individual, while I enjoyed a few moments of solitude at the table. That's when my eyes were drawn to a couple standing near the back wall, holding hands and smiling at each other, obviously lost in a very private moment. He was in uniform; she was wearing boots and jeans. When they turned to speak to another deputy, I recognized Sergeant Steve Owen and his wife, Detective Tania Owen.

I was acquainted with Steve because he worked with Mitch, and though I'd seen Tania a few times, we'd never met. In my eyes, she was always one of the most beautiful and striking women I'd ever seen. I couldn't help but smile as I watched them, still holding hands, walk toward a group of deputies standing together near the bar area, Steve's chest puffed out with obvious pride because of the woman at his side. I remember thinking, *God, how he loves his wife,* and my heart just melted.

A short time later I was still seated at the table and talking with a guest when I felt a hand on my shoulder. I turned and saw Steve Owen smiling down at me. "Hey, Vickie, I have to go back on patrol now, but I wanted to come say hello—and give you a hug." Steve took my hand as I stood and then happily moved into his brotherly embrace. I can only describe that hug as the biggest bear hug I'd received in my life, and when I stepped back and looked into Steve's eyes, they were filled with tears.

"Vickie, I'm so sorry for what you, Mitch, and your family are going through right now. If there was any way I could take this cancer from Mitch, I'd do it in a second. I want you to promise me something, okay?"

"Sure, Steve, what is it?"

"If there's anything—*anything*—either Tania or I can do, please let me know."

I promised I would, and then he said, "I don't think you've met Tania," who'd been standing a few respectful feet away, a smile on her face. He introduced us, and we shared a handshake I'll never forget. I thanked them both for being there, and we said goodbye.

Later that night, as Mitch and I drove home from the event, I was still moved by Steve Owen's tears. Mitch had always described him as the "John Wayne of cops," because he had the reputation of being larger than life. But I'd just seen another side of him, and when I told Mitch what Steve had said about taking the cancer if he could, Mitch also shed a tear.

Though Mitch had initially sailed through chemo, as he neared the completion of the round, he hit a rough spot. After a couple of tough days, I knew it was time to have another heart-to-heart talk with him.

"Mitch, I have a question for you."

"Sure, what is it?"

"What do you need from me at this point in the treatment process? What can I do for you? Maybe I should be at home more."

Despite the physical struggle he was dealing with that week, Mitch's answer didn't surprise me: "I need you to go to work every day and live life like normal. If I need you, I'll let you know. I promise."

"But, Mitch, I hate being at work when I know you're struggling."

"No 'buts' Vickie. You and I have lived long enough and gone through enough challenges to know that life sometimes deals us blows. Didn't we recently tell Brodie he was to enter his master's program as scheduled? He's still a young man, and we need to be deliberate in how we live life and demonstrate our faith to him and others right now."

I knew Mitch was right. I'd held my position at the construction company for more than ten years, and I had no need to prove myself. The owners of the company knew and loved Mitch; they'd already assured me of their support. I just needed to take a deep breath and follow the Bible lesson from 1 Peter 5:7 that our pastor had illuminated the previous Sunday: cast all your care on Him, for He cares for you.

That's just what I was doing the afternoon of the first Wednesday in October as I ran numbers on our company's latest commercial project. My thoughts were interrupted when I heard one of my coworkers say, "Oh my gosh! My daughter just texted me that her elementary school is on lockdown." I didn't think much of it since lockdown was a routine protective response anytime something happened in the area of a school.

Just then my phone dinged with a text from Mitch: *A sergeant has been shot. You need to start praying.* Before I could respond, I heard my coworker say, "There's been a shooting!"

I quickly texted Mitch: *What's going on?* A moment later he responded with *Steve Owen's been shot. Vic, he's not going to make it—you need to drop to your knees now!*

Though Mitch's professional status was IOD (injured on duty), he was still an active detective. At that moment I didn't know if he was at home or somewhere else. What I did know with certainty is that Mitch would choose to be at the hospital with his law enforcement family, and my immediate concern was that he was okay.

I tried to reach him for the next twenty minutes, but he neither responded to my texts nor answered my calls.

At this point, I was deeply concerned for everyone; for all I knew, more than one deputy had been injured. I grabbed my purse and went to my boss's office, "I have to go; I need to get to the hospital."

My mind was racing as I sped toward Antelope Valley Hospital, my thoughts turning to Steve's wife, Tania, whom I'd met only ten days ago. I was aware that because she was a deputy, the department was already surrounding her, but what of their adult children? With the advent of social media, it was no longer possible to withhold the release of bad news while families were notified. *Oh, God, please be with the Owen family and protect them,* I prayed silently.

As I pulled into the hospital parking lot, my sole focus was finding my husband so that I could be there for him. But as I looked at the sea of black-and-white vehicles, lights flashing, and literally hundreds of uniformed deputies and officers keeping people from entering the hospital, I had no idea how I would find Mitch.

I thanked God when two deputies from the Lancaster Station recognized me and said they'd take me to Mitch. They escorted me down a long hallway lined with uniformed men and women, all standing eerily quiet, toward the entrance to the chapel. Mitch saw me before I saw him. He was running toward me, his eyes locked on mine as I instinctively dropped my purse and he stepped into my arms, sobbing. He didn't need to say a word, and I didn't have to ask. Steve Owen was gone.

A palpable presence of disbelief and grief had descended like a fog both inside and outside the hospital. For the next few hours, I was amazed at the inner strength Mitch had somehow tapped into, enabling us to show love and provide comfort to other deputies in the face of this unimaginable loss.

At some point we stepped into the chapel, where Steve Owen's flag-draped body was surrounded by dozens of uniformed deputies. While Mitch spoke quietly with a group of deputies from the Lancaster Station, my gazed turned to Tania Owen, seated with her daughter and one son as they waited for the other son to arrive from out of town. I could not imagine the horror Tania and her family had experienced—and were still experiencing. As a law-enforcement wife, my heart broke for this woman, yet I was struck by her calm demeanor and the sense of peace that surrounded her.

Mitch and I left the hospital around 9:00 p.m. Though he wanted to be part of the escort that transported Steve's body to Los Angeles, he was physically exhausted. Lying in bed beside me that night, Mitch gave me the account of what he'd learned about the events of the afternoon, how Steve had been shot after answering a burglary call. Then he said, "Vickie, when we talk about Steve, we must never say he was killed in the line of duty. He wasn't killed—he was murdered. There's a difference. When someone intentionally does what that man did to Steve, it's murder. And that's what we will call it from this time forward."

My heart was heavy the next morning when I went back to work. Despite yesterday being a long day, Mitch went to the station. The next few days were a media circus in Lancaster; the entire city seemed to be on lockdown as the national media descended on our community and Antelope Valley's residents remained glued to their televisions. I was pleased when Mitch told me the Owen family had decided to leave town together for a couple of days.

As I prepared dinner one evening the following week, waiting for Mitch to come home from the station, I had a conversation with God. *Lord, this horrible loss of Steve Owen has shown me that life can change in an instant. I don't know how much time Mitch and I have together, but I want more than anything to honor him and love him. I'm asking you to help me and to show me how to do it.*

Just then I heard Mitch's vehicle pull in the driveway, and a moment later he walked in the door. I'd been concerned he was pushing himself too much, yet tonight he seemed different; his countenance was a bit brighter. As a detective Mitch had gone to the station today for the scheduled debriefing about Steve's murder. I set aside the salad bowl, wiped my hands on a towel, and gave him a hug. "Hi, honey. How was the debriefing?"

"That's actually what I want to talk to you about. How long before dinner?"

"About forty minutes. How about we sit down and have a glass of tea?"

Mitch told me the debriefing room had been packed with deputies. Tania and her children—Chadd, Tyler, and Shannon—had been there, as well as Steve's mother, Millie. Mitch then shared the awful details of the events surrounding Steve's murder, as well as the facts that had come to light in the subsequent investigation.

"Oh, Mitch, that had to be so difficult for everyone—especially Tania and the family. Is she okay?"

"I'll let you decide after I tell you what happened next." Now he really had my attention. "After the debriefing the lieutenant asked Tania if she'd like to speak. At first she said no, but then she changed her mind—you could have heard a pin drop as she went to the front of the room." Mitch smiled as he continued. "Tania could see how badly everyone was hurting, and she basically told us we had to snap out of it. She said she wouldn't allow any 'what if' thinking because the truth was, Steve was where he wanted to be: at home with Jesus."

"She actually said that?" I asked.

"Oh, it gets better, Vic. She told us that two days before Steve was murdered, they'd had a conversation about what they would do if something ever happened to either of them. They agreed that after one year, the other one would be free to move forward with his or her life. However, she said she knew Steve couldn't wait that long, and told him if he wanted to move forward sooner, he could. But then she told him that if he brought another woman into *their* house, she'd come back and haunt him."

"Mitch, are you just kidding with me?"

"No, Vickie, that's exactly what she said. But strange as it sounds, she made everyone laugh, and when she did, the heaviness in that room lifted. At that point she sounded more like a preacher than a deputy. She challenged anyone who was dealing with anger, fear, or any deadly emotion to give it to God and then receive the same peace she had. Finally, she invited everyone to attend church with her this coming Sunday. I'm telling you, the hour she spoke was a powerful experience for everyone."

"What an amazing woman she is, Mitch. I'm so happy I had the opportunity to meet her, and I hope that once we get past this horror, I can talk with her again."

"Well, maybe you'll have that chance this Sunday at her church. We need to be there to love and support the Owen family, and I know a lot of the deputies are planning to go."

The following Sunday Mitch and I attended Steve and Tania's church, The Road Church of the Antelope Valley. I felt a bit uncomfortable not being in our home church, where we'd found the help needed to turn our marriage around when we'd hit a rough spot six years earlier. Though The Road was smaller and more casual than what I was accustomed, the people were genuinely friendly, the praise and worship refreshing and uplifting. Mitch was especially happy to see so many of his fellow deputies in attendance.

On the way home from church, Mitch told me he'd been asked to sing at Steve's funeral, scheduled for the upcoming Thursday. He was so honored he'd been asked; however, having just completed chemo, he wasn't sure he was physically able to sing. In the end he decided to try, believing that singing "American Lawman" in honor of Sergeant Steve Owen would be the most important thing he could do for the Owen family.

As it turned out, his rich baritone voice set the stage for the beautiful service that unified our community in honoring Steve Owen—amazing husband, father, and deputy—while giving glory to God.

In retrospect, Mitch had no idea his decision to sing that day would mark a defining moment for the Owen and Speed families, whom God was bringing together for a purpose yet to be revealed.

The following Sunday morning I was surprised when Mitch said we'd be attending church at The Road again. I remember thinking, *That wasn't our deal. We were supposed to go once to support the Owen family.* But we went again, and Mitch wasted no time in jumping right in, talking to the deputies he knew and other people he'd never met. He even made a point to meet the members of the worship team. I could see he was happy to be there, but I was ready to go back to the familiarity of our home church.

When we got into our vehicle to go home, I turned to Mitch and said, "We're going back to our church next weekend." It wasn't really a question; it was more of a statement.

"Well, Vic, I really like this church," Mitch said.

"Okay," I said, "You can stay here, but I'm going back to our church."

That's when I clearly heard the voice of the Lord in my spirit: *"Well, that wasn't very honoring, was it?"* Uh-oh. Hadn't I just last week asked the Lord to help me to honor and love my husband? So I said, "I'm sorry Mitch. If you want to come back here, then I'll come with you."

I didn't want to change churches, but I knew in my heart that married couples needed to be in church *together*. I was determined to honor my husband; therefore, relinquishing my need to be in control was the right thing to do.

And as it turned out, I fell in love with The Road Church of the Antelope Valley. By December of 2016, Mitch was responding well to his treatment; his PSA levels were amazing. When he'd been diagnosed, his number was 194. Following chemotherapy, it had dropped to 0.2.

MARCH 2016

We celebrated Christmas with full expectation Mitch was going to beat this. After all, our family was "Speed Strong."

Chapter Four

THE BUCKET LIST

Vickie Speed

Under the leadership of Pastors John Santero and Jason Grundy, Mitch absolutely flourished at The Road. He especially identified with John Santero, an active captain with the Los Angeles County Fire Department who had more than three decades of service under his belt.

Many people in our community knew Mitch was a singer, so it wasn't surprising he was invited to sing one Sunday. He soon became a permanent member of the worship team, which had been a lifelong dream for him.

It made me happy to see how much joy Mitch experienced from being part of this church and the strength he derived from that joy.

Not surprising, since the Bible says, *For the joy of the* LORD *is your strength* (Nehemiah 8:10).

We were both thankful that Tania Owen had extended the initial invitation for Lancaster Station deputies to attend church with her following Steve's murder, and we now saw her most Sundays. Having worked with Steve and Tania for years, Mitch was acquainted with their three children. Our son, Brodie, had been friends with Tyler Owen in school, and Mitch and I had known Chadd Owen's wife, Nicole, for years before they married. Though I'd only recently met Tania, our families clearly had some well-established ties.

Mitch was viewed as a father figure, not only to the younger deputies but also to the young people in our community. It was only natural that he would take special interest in Steve and Tania's children, despite the fact they were adults leading their own lives. "Vickie, I want to do what I can to love and support the Owen family," he told me one day. "I've asked God to show me how I can be an encouragement to each one of them." I loved how, though dealing with a cancer diagnosis, Mitch remained focused on others, on meeting their needs. My husband truly lived his faith in front of those he came in contact with.

Mitch regularly talked to Steve and Tania's children on the phone; he also sent frequent texts with words of encouragement and Bible verses. Because Chadd and Shannon lived nearby, they often visited Mitch.

Several months had passed since Steve's murder, yet attention from the news media remained unrelenting. They used any means in an effort to get an interview with Tania or her family.

Tania told us that people who didn't even know Steve often approached their children, saying, "We know your mom," which was particularly upsetting for Shannon because she knew they didn't. In a world where the Owen family had to be careful about whom to trust, Mitch became a safe place for Chadd, Tyler, and Shannon. Chadd often referred to Mitch as "my new earthly dad." To Shannon he was "Uncle Mitch."

Though we'd recently learned that blood clots had formed in Mitch's arm and leg, we didn't make the information public. There wasn't a day Mitch didn't have a smile on his face or wasn't happy. He was determined to live his life to the fullest.

I had honored my husband's request to go to work every day and live life as normally as possible. Oftentimes while I was poring over construction figures at my office, I would smile as I envisioned him at home taking care of himself, perhaps lying on the sofa in front of the television while texting the Owen family. Unbeknownst to me, he was driving to the nearby junior college track field, where he walked three days a week.

Mitch's healthcare team had encouraged him to walk; however, I'm not sure his chosen method was exactly what they'd intended. In just a short time he was joined each day by anywhere from two to twenty people—some, deputies in uniform—who were there for fellowship and to hear Mitch's words of faith and encouragement. As the group grew and gained public attention, they chose for themselves the name *Speed Walkers*.

On the days he wasn't walking at the college, Mitch was often at the Lancaster Station, mentoring, encouraging, and laughing with the men and women he considered his brothers and sisters. I don't recall exactly when it happened, but at some point, I realized my husband was giving birth to a ministry—and my sense was that it would make an impact on many people.

Though Mitch was strong and vibrant in spirit, the same was not true with his body. My husband—the strong, 6'3" badass cop-cowboy—wasn't so strong anymore. He was in the fight of his life. But it seemed the more intense the battle became, the stronger I got. I remember telling myself, *God really made me to do this, and I know I can do it.*

I became Mitch's protector as I took responsibility for our finances, our home, and anything that concerned our son. At Mitch's insistence Brodie was now in his master's program at the University of San Francisco's satellite campus in Anaheim. Never for one minute did I resent not having a choice in the matter of managing our lives. I assumed the role because I loved my husband, because it's what a spouse is supposed to do. During that time, I would often open my Bible to 2 Corinthians 9 and take comfort in the word the Lord spoke to the apostle Paul: *"My grace is sufficient for you, for My strength is made perfect in weakness"* (verse 9).

One spring evening as Mitch and I sat together in our courtyard, he talked about things he'd wanted to accomplish, things he'd put on the back burner for years while focusing on his career in law enforcement. In essence he'd put together his own bucket list of dreams he wanted to fulfill before the end of the year. In my mind, even for a healthy person, the list was overwhelming, and I told him so. But then Mitch opened his Bible and read two particular verses to me: *I can do all things through Christ who strengthens me* (Philippians 4:13), and *But Jesus looked at them and said to them,*

"With men this is impossible, but with God all things are possible" (Matthew 19:26).

Who was I to argue with the Word of God? I made up my mind right then that I would honor my husband by supporting him any way I could in accomplishing his goals.

Mentoring others was important to Mitch, and prior to his diagnosis he'd volunteered as an assistant football coach at his alma mater, Rosamond High School. Many of the boys on the team were growing up as Mitch had, raised by a single mother without a father figure, and he wanted to be there for them. Though having to step down from coaching was a setback for him, Mitch continued to meet with three or four of the young men he'd become particularly close to. He and a small group of retired businessmen, deputies, and firefighters—who named themselves *Iron Sharpens Iron*—worked with at-risk youth who couldn't attend public schools because of behavioral issues. Instead they helped to connect these young people with the *Opportunities for Learning* network of charter high schools in Southern California.

Practically speaking, there were neither enough hours in the week, nor did Mitch have the ability to impact young people in a significant way on a one-on-one basis. That's when an idea occurred to him. He'd been using social media to communicate with the Owen family between times of personal contact; why not use it to connect with people of all ages who were hungry for encouragement?

Mitch had been writing since high school. As long as I'd known him, writing had been his means of dealing with feelings and emotions. Between his creative writing and his ability as a singer, he had plenty of material to post on a daily basis, and that's exactly what he did. Within a very short period of time, he had a huge following, which opened the door for the big-ticket item on Mitch's bucket list: a book.

Throughout the summer months Mitch was fully engaged with the book project, spending hours each day at his computer. And yet he still made time for his daily social media posts, mentoring, visiting the Lancaster Station twice each week, and—of course—helping to lead praise and worship each Sunday at church.

I always accompanied him to his appointments at the City of Hope, where the continual scans and MRIs—routine to us now—confirmed the cancer's progression. At one point Mitch said, "Vic, sometimes I feel like I can't catch a break with this thing. It's like I take the proverbial one step forward, two steps backwards." Still, the medical team had not run out of treatment options, so we continued to remain "Speed Strong."

One of the high points of 2017 came with the release of Mitch's book in October. Titled *Mitch Speed—The Man Behind the Badge*, it was a collection of stories Mitch had penned about his real-life experiences and the values that had made him who he was. Also included in the book were more than a dozen poems he'd written throughout the years. Some were humorous, some were filled with wisdom, and some spoke vital truth directly to matters of the human heart.

Mitch was so excited when the first shipment of books arrived at the house. He had presold dozens of copies, sales he'd carefully recorded on a spread sheet. Now the books had to be individually packaged and shipped to readers eagerly awaiting their arrival.

Mitch did all of this on his own, carefully hand signing each book with his distinguishable autograph: "Be blessed, —Mitch—"

The book was an immediate success, selling over one thousand copies in the first run. The first book-signing event was scheduled at the Palmdale Barnes and Noble, and we had no idea how many people might show up. As it turned out, people waited patiently for two hours in a line that ran through the store and out the front door. In addition to seeing people he'd grown up with, Mitch's high school English teacher was there to congratulate him and get a signed copy of his book.

After our local newspaper, the *Antelope Valley Press*, did a story about the book and Mitch's battle with cancer, even more people showed up at the second Barnes and Noble book signing, this one in nearby Santa Clarita. Customers pulling into the parking lot that morning encountered a line of sheriff's vehicles outside the big double-door entrance, their lights flashing, and uniformed deputies welcoming them to the book signing.

Despite the joy Mitch experienced that day, I knew he was in constant pain as he shared a kind word with each person in line and thanked them for buying his book. I'd learned living with cancer was like a rollercoaster ride. You can wake up and have breakfast together and everything be wonderful. But within two hours you may need to call for an ambulance.

The downside of the rollercoaster ride came at our next appointment with Mitch's oncologist, Dr. M. Houman Fekrazad. That's when we learned the treatment strategy had changed. The latest scans and MRIs confirmed the cancer remained active; therefore, the medical focus was to control the cancer, to slow it down. The next step was radiation.

Mitch was to undergo treatments five days a week, for nine weeks. Just prior to starting the treatments, we agreed it was now time for me to make a significant adjustment in my work schedule. I still went to the office each morning, but I now left at 1:00 p.m., after which I took Mitch to his treatments. I'm so thankful that not one time over those nine weeks were there less than fifty deputies waiting at the City of Hope's front doors to pray for us before we entered. This amazing demonstration of how much my husband was loved always gave me strength.

There's no way to adequately describe the effects of radiation. Though capable of diagnosing and treating the disease, the aftermath of the treatment was brutal. It became clear to me that my husband was failing, which meant cancer was taking the lead. As we approached the end of 2017, I was determined to make Thanksgiving and Christmas at the Speed house the most beautiful and meaningful ever.

The unmistakable aroma of roasting turkey filled our home Thanksgiving Day as some twenty family members and friends joined us to watch football and enjoy the annual feast. I wasn't prepared for the looks of concern on our guests' faces. Those who hadn't seen Mitch for a while were understandably stunned by the drastic change in his appearance. The day was physically difficult for Mitch, but we were both happy to be surrounded by those we loved.

No sooner had Thanksgiving come and gone than I began decorating for Christmas. Mitch was physically unable to help with the process; however, he played a significant role in our annual Christmas communication with family and friends with this beautiful letter:

December 2017

Dear family and friends,

Today I am thankful for the gift in my life. I am thankful for the gift of opening my eyes to another morning. I am thankful for the gift of a wife and a son who are truly heaven sent. I am thankful for my friends and family. And I am thankful for the journey and the gift of clarity. Clarity to understand that life is not measured by ribbons and bows and presents. No, life is measured by the love and the "presence" of friends and family.

I am thankful for finally understanding that life is about living for Him. As I sit here and look at our Christmas tree, I am drawn to the angel on top of our tree. The same angel that was a gift from my mother so many years ago. My mother who taught me that love for one another is truly a gift. My mother who taught me that true fulfillment can only be found when we are willing to give our life to Him and to love one another.

I look at the decorations and I see remnants of my son's childhood. And in these remnants, I am reminded of the love I have shared with Vickie and Brodie. I am reminded of the Christmases we have shared together and the life we have built together. I am reminded that *that* little boy has grown into a man who fills my heart with pride and joy. My son understands the love of God and the gift that God has given him.

I look at Vickie and know that I have been blessed with a woman who loves me more than I love myself. She is my rock, and she continues to hold my hand as we walk along the path of this journey God has put before us. I am thankful that God guides us as we learn more and more about His love and the purpose we must serve.

And I am thankful that God has shown me how to walk with a thankful heart, even in what may appear to be a tough time. He has given me the strength to stand and breathe. He has given me knowledge, and He continues to place the words in my heart to share with you all.

So, thank you, God. Thank you for showing us your love. Thank you for never giving up on us, even when we turn away from you. Thank you for the gift of today.

Be blessed,
—Mitch—

Christmas in the Speed house had always been a private celebration for just the three of us: Mitch, Brodie, and me. For me Christmas Day was the day I spoiled my boys—and this year was no exception. The house was decorated from top to bottom, not a tree or shrub in the front yard was without a light, and over the past two weeks, the three of us had watched every movie from *It's a Wonderful Life* to *Christmas Story* to *Polar Express* for the umpteenth time. Mitch's pain was under control, and there was a light in his eyes as he handed me my Christmas gift.

I carefully untied the ribbon and opened the box—to find yet another wrapped box inside; this one a small, black velvet box. I gasped when I opened it, and when my eyes met Mitch's, I knew we were both remembering a certain walk we'd taken on the beach on August 24, 2016, our twenty-fifth wedding anniversary.

Prior to Mitch's diagnosis, we'd planned to renew our vows that year, and Mitch had been adamant about buying me a new ring. Though we didn't have much money when we married, I'd always loved the simple gold band with diamonds that I'd worn for the past twenty-five years. "Mitch, I really don't need a new wedding ring," I'd insisted.

"Well, Vic, you can either agree to go with me to the jewelry store, or I'll have to go alone and select one myself." Of course, I'd agreed to go shopping with him, and for the next several weeks we'd done a lot of window shopping at jewelry stores.

But once Mitch was diagnosed with cancer, we had put those plans on hold, not knowing how the coming months would unfold. Instead, we'd celebrated our twenty-fifth anniversary with a walk on the beach, where we'd reflected on our life together and spoken of future dreams.

And now—a little more than a year after taking that anniversary walk together—my husband had purchased the very ring I'd most loved and was placing it on my finger this Christmas morning. How was it possible for my heart to be so full, and yet at the same time breaking?

I think Mitch and I both knew this was our last Christmas together.

At our first appointment at the City of Hope in January 2018, we learned Mitch's numbers were tripling every twenty-eight days and the cancer was now in his bones. The doctor told us they were going to try a new medication; however, at this point they were running out of options. In other words, Mitch was in serious trouble.

In true Mitch fashion, he accepted the news with grace and then asked me to take a photo of him with Dr. Fekrazad. Both men were smiling. Later that day, Mitch posted the photo with a note saying how grateful he was for the City of Hope and its amazing medical staff.

Throughout our nearly two-year journey people had often told me they couldn't believe Mitch was dealing with cancer; he looked so good and was always so happy. That's because we'd chosen to keep the battle at home, to never allow it to be the center of our lives. Mitch remained adamant in wanting the world to see him as a man who lived life to the fullest—even in the face of cancer. As for me I'd decided early on I would not live in fear of death. That decision—and my absolute faith in God—is what kept me strong.

If asked to identify the most important truth I learned throughout the battle, I'd have to say it's this: God uniquely designed and equipped women—as wives and mothers—to be the glue in our families. Perhaps that's why, when the religious leaders of the day challenged Jesus about marriage, He said, *"Have you not read that*

He who made them at the beginning 'made them male and female,' and said, 'For this reason a man shall leave his father and mother and be joined to his wife, and the two shall become one flesh'? So then, they are no longer two but one flesh. Therefore what God has joined together, let not man separate" (Matthew 12:4–6).

Though I was spiritually, emotionally, and physically prepared for the battle ahead, the days that followed weren't easy. Up to that point I'd never cried, but then Mitch took a turn in April. The pain caused by the cancer in his bones was so severe that he was hospitalized for several days to get it under control. That's when I broke; however, I refused to cry in front of my husband and son. Determined to remain strong for the two people I loved most, I poured out my heart and tears to God in the daily privacy and safety of my shower stall.

Brodie was to receive his master's degree from the University of San Francisco on May 18, and I struggled to figure out how to be there for him and yet leave Mitch at home. There was no way I'd make the more than three-hundred-mile trip in my car, so I decided to fly. As it turned out, Mitch was feeling better the week of graduation, so we made arrangements for several deputies to stay with him. Knowing Mitch's "brothers" would be there round the clock to ensure everything was okay was a great comfort to me.

I had total peace about the plan—until ten minutes before I was to leave for the airport and the toilet in our front bathroom overflowed. I had no choice but to leave the matter in the hands of the deputies who, by the time I was ready to board my flight, had already shut off the water, cleaned the floor, purchased a new toilet, and were preparing to install it.

Brodie's graduation was live streamed that day, so Mitch was able to watch our son receive his master's degree in sports management, with a minor in kinesiology. Of course, Mitch and I were texting back and forth throughout the ceremony. At one point he told me, "I feel like I'm there. I'm so excited I get to see him."

I was comforted to know Mitch's fellow deputies were there with him at home. Throughout the entire journey, anytime we had a need or required assistance there were between two and six black and whites in front of our house. This was the case the final week of May when, one day, Mitch's pain became so bad, I had to call 911. We'd agreed not to make public the fact that the cancer in his bones was so advanced that his spine could actually snap.

The ambulance arrived within minutes, and once Mitch had been carefully loaded inside, the accompanying sheriff's vehicles made sure all intersections remained blocked so that we could get to the Antelope Valley Hospital without delay. Seated in the front of the ambulance, I remember thinking, *My God, this man is so loved.*

It took a full ten, difficult days to get Mitch's pain under control, and the staff at the Antelope Valley Hospital couldn't have been kinder to us throughout the process. However, one day while Steve and Tania Owen's daughter, Shannon, was visiting, Mitch wasn't given his meds on schedule, and he was experiencing a lot of pain. That's when I saw a side of Shannon I'd never before experienced. She took charge of the situation, went to the nurses' desk to speak with the individual in charge, and within minutes the matter was taken care of. As the saying goes, you can't catch lightning in a bottle—but in my mind Shannon Owen had just proved that saying wrong.

I'd slept at the hospital nightly until the final night, just prior to Mitch's release. Before I left that evening, the hospital staff explained that because he was taking what, for most people, was an excessive amount of medication, the only way they could release Mitch to return home was if he was under hospice care. This was the first time anyone had mentioned hospice. *Okay, it's just a technicality to get him home; this isn't the end,* I reasoned to myself as I drove home.

When I came back the following morning, June 8, Mitch shared some disappointing news: he'd taken a fall while I'd been gone. "I don't know what happened, Vic, but when I tried to stand up, my legs gave out." I knew he was weak; I just hadn't realized how weak.

The minute we got into the car to go home, Mitch grabbed my hand and said, "Vic, please don't bring me back here again. I don't want to be in the hospital anymore—I want to go home."

"Okay, Mitch, we're going home right now," I said. And then I wondered, *Did he mean he wants to go home to our house or home to be with Jesus?*

When I turned onto our street a short time later, it was lined on both sides with black and whites, and our yard filled with deputies who'd come to help move Mitch inside. Their presence gave me strength as I steeled myself for the inevitable changes to come, the most significant being the wheelchair Mitch was required to use to move about.

Brodie was home on a permanent basis, and our friend and physician's assistant, Stephanie, had come to stay with us. Within three days Mitch had completely lost the use of his legs, rendering him virtually bedridden as the cancer continued to wear away his bones.

Absolutely determined my husband was *not* going to spend his days and nights secluded in our bedroom, I came up with an idea.

Our home had an open floor plan, so why not convert our dining area into a bedroom and make the adjoining living area a place where friends and family could gather and be comfortable? One of the deputies Mitch knew from the courts was married to the manager of the Sleep Number store. She was more than happy to make sure we got the perfect bed. While I was about it, with the help of a girlfriend, Valerie, I also purchased additional new furniture as well as some beautiful rugs and other designer items.

The day we moved everything in felt as if we were filming an episode of *Fixer Upper*. A team of off-duty deputies removed the old furnishings and brought in the new—including a brand-new big-screen TV they hung on the wall. In just a little under four hours, our home had been transformed.

Several of the deputies had moved Mitch to the new bed, where he happily played with the remote controls, alternately adjusting the bed and changing the stations on the TV. As I made the finishing touches, placing family photos where Mitch could see them, I realized how happy he was to be right in the heart of our home's activity.

That night, after he'd received his pain medication and we were lying on the new Sleep Number mattress watching television, Mitch said, "Hey, Vickie, do you remember when Steve Owen told Tania that if he died she should wait a year to move on?"

I figured the pain meds were speaking. "Yeah, but why are you asking me about that?"

"Well, you don't have to wait a year."

Immediately I burst into tears. "How can you talk to me like that right now? I don't want you to go, and I certainly don't want to have this conversation. I can't *imagine* my life without you, Mitch!"

He was quiet for a moment, and I thought maybe he'd drop the subject; better yet, maybe he'd go to sleep. But then he turned toward me, placed his hand ever so tenderly on my face and said, "Babe, let me just enlighten you. If the shoe were on the other foot, you need to understand I'd have a girlfriend within two or three months."

Needless to say, that little revelation certainly snapped me out of my morose moment. I wiped my eyes and cleared my throat. "Well, Mitch, let *me* just enlighten *you* about something. Considering the fact that you require my constant help for pretty much everything you need or want to do right now, you're not really in a position to make me mad."

"Vic, I'm not trying to make you mad. I just want to be honest with you. Think about it: you'd be dead, and I'd have a girlfriend."

By then we were both laughing. "So it sounds as if you've given the matter quite a bit of thought," I said.

"I'm not saying I'd get married, but I'd for sure have a girlfriend. After all, the guys are accustomed to my having a beautiful wife—it wouldn't be right for them to see me without some female eye candy. Can you imagine the looks on their faces if I showed up with a twenty-five-year-old?"

"Mitch, you have no idea what I'm imagining right now."

"Well, I'm glad you finally see my point. So, Vickie, you don't need to wait a year. You have my permission to move forward, because I know there will be a line of guys around the block just waiting to date you."

"Whatever, Mitch," I said, rolling my eyes.

I held my husband's hand as he drifted off to sleep. As I lay there looking at the man whose bed I'd shared for the past twenty-eight years, I remembered the day, twenty-four months earlier, when Mitch told me we wouldn't be able to have sex again. I was so thankful for the miracle God had performed in me: He'd removed every ounce of my sexual desire and had replaced it with a love for my husband I'd never before experienced. It was something I wouldn't trade for anything.

There would be no more doctor's appointments, no more visits to the City of Hope; Mitch was now under hospice care. I took a leave of absence from work so that I could be with my husband in what I knew would be his final weeks.

In addition to experiencing constant pain, Mitch was frustrated that he was confined to the bed. And yet, he remained ever the prayer warrior in behalf of his family and friends. The stream of visitors was constant; we all knew each person who came to our home loved Mitch and they were coming to say goodbye. Most visitors would ask Mitch how he was doing, to which he always replied, "I'm doing great—let me pray for you."

On Father's Day, June 17, Brodie and Mitch spent the day together. Knowing Mitch wanted to speak some things to Brodie that were for our son's ears only, I gave them their space. As a father, Mitch wanted to talk to Brodie about his life, how to move forward and be the man God created him to be and how to be a husband

and father. It was a day Brodie will never forget and one for which I'm eternally grateful.

Mitch and I had our private conversation a few days later, and it was surprisingly practical. We talked about finances, our son's future, and Mitch's wishes for how he wanted us to move forward. Mitch talked to me about the next chapter of my life. "We've had an incredible chapter together, Vickie, and you should always remember it and hold on to it. But I want nothing more for you than for your next chapter to be equally incredible."

I told Mitch how grateful I was for the life he'd given me, how blessed I was that he'd chosen me to be his wife and share this journey with him. I told him I thanked God for choosing me to take care of him during this difficult time and to be there at his side.

Thanks to Mitch's excellent financial planning over the years, I wouldn't *need* to return to work, but I wanted to know what he thought I should do: return to work or focus on being a mother to Brodie (though he was a grown man). Most importantly, I wanted to know how in the world I could move on with my life without my husband.

In true Mitch Speed fashion, he didn't directly answer my questions; rather, he gave me the words I needed to guide me to the right decisions: "Vic, you have to find your purpose and then let your purpose be bigger than your pain."

At the end of June, Mitch looked into my eyes and said, "Vic, I've fought the good fight, and I'm ready to go home." He asked me to hand him his copy of *The Message,* lying open on the bedside table, from which he read John 3:30: *"That's why my cup is running over. This is the assigned moment for him to move to the center, while I slip off to the sidelines."*

Mitch then asked my permission for him to go home. He needed that support from me, and I knew it was time. He'd fought as hard as he could, and I'd remained strong in his behalf. But I loved him enough to let him go, and so I told him he had my permission to go.

The following week our pastor, John Santero, came to the house to pray for Mitch, but Mitch would have none of it. "Oh, no, John. I have to pray for you. I know where I'm going, brother, but you're being left in this world—so let me pray for you." And that's just what Mitch did. In fact, though he was weak, he still prayed for every visitor who stepped into our home—many of whom wept openly at their last goodbyes.

Mitch's heaviest burden was the idea of leaving his family behind. He made Brodie and I promise we would not allow his passing to fill us with tears; rather, that we would rejoice because he would be home with his family: Mom, Papa, and his brother, Bill, all of whom had gone before him. He so looked forward to being with them again. Mitch wasn't sad and he wasn't angry; he was at perfect peace, knowing he would soon be in heaven.

A few days later Mitch told me of a dream he'd had. In it, his mother was busy preparing a bed for him, and he'd been excited to see her. "Vic, I'm so looking forward to seeing Mom," he told me. "I really miss her." Though I didn't want to hear that his focus was transitioning to where he was soon going, I was happy for him. I was also grateful that, six years ago, God had repaired our once-broken marriage and given us these beautiful years together. I had absolutely no regrets.

Though God had blessed me with strength beyond my expectation for the past twenty-six months, watching Mitch suffer through unimaginable pain literally dropped me. Now when I cried in the shower, I no longer asked for strength; instead, I begged God to take him home. My husband was so very frail, and all I wanted to do was protect him and let him leave this world with dignity. That's why I made the decision to stop all visitation. I didn't want people to remember Mitch as the man with cancer; I wanted them to remember Mitch Speed the man, the true warrior.

The morning of July 4, 2018, I knew something was different. On the day when he would normally have been singing the national anthem at the City of Lancaster's Independence Day celebration, Mitch began his transition to heaven, entering a comatose state.

For the next three days, he was medicated every ninety minutes. On the morning of July 7, Stephanie—who was staying with me—said his passing was eminent. Then at 9:35 p.m., Brodie and I each holding one of his hands, Mitch took his final breath. In an instant the room was permeated with the most amazing sense of peace, and I knew the pain had ended; Mitch was now healed and at home in the arms of Jesus.

Before I made the necessary notifications, Brodie and I shared our final private moments together with the man who'd been the love of my life and Brodie's hero. Within the hour our house was filled with friends who'd come to comfort and pray for us.

When Mitch's body was moved from our home to the coroner's vehicle, both sides of our sidewalk were lined with sheriff's deputies standing at attention. Mitch had been adamant that we not shed tears—for all of us, a task easier said than done. But then, something curious happened: Mitch's phone sounded the familiar ding that signaled a text message. It was from Chadd Owen:

> Mitch, I know you are in heaven, but I need to get this in words. Thank you for being a dad to me when I lost mine. I honestly have no idea how I would have made it without you and Vickie. You guys were my rock when I needed one, and you had a home to let me vent without judgment. I dreaded the day you would be gone, but when I found out the news that you had gone home, my heart was comforted. You are no longer in pain, and you are with our Lord and Savior, Jesus! You touched so many lives and fulfilled God's purpose. Well done good and faithful servant. I will carry the torch and keep your mission going. Bible study will keep going! I will always be here for Vickie and Brodie in whatever they need. Thank you for all that you have done for me and my family. Until we meet again … I love you, Mitch!
>
> Chadd Owen

The phone continued to ding while I read Chadd's message; obviously, the news about Mitch's passing had been circulated on social media. The messages continued to come in.

> "Thank you" doesn't feel like a big enough gesture for you, Mitch, but thank you for the memories of working patrol. Thank you for being the embodiment of a great husband and father. Thank you for believing in me, even in times

when I doubted myself. Thank you for sharing your faith with others. Thank you for your guidance, advice, strength, and strong words when your brothers and sisters needed them most. Thank you for the laughs we shared. Most of all, thank you for being my friend. God bless you, Mitch—J.F.

Hey Buddy ... I know you are now in heaven, and God has another angel's beautiful voice. Thank you for being such a wonderful inspiration in what it means to be a Christian, husband, father, and friend. We will all miss you and will do our best to take care of your family—B.D.

You are going to be greatly missed, Mitch. You left a mark on this earth most can't achieve. How blessed you were to be chosen by the Lord to spread the word and touch so many lives. You will always be loved and forever in our hearts. I love you—J.K.

Mitch, I just heard the news that you took your last walk. I guess all of those miles we walked together came in handy. You felt like an older brother, and you taught me more than you know. You helped push me to be a better father to my boys. My friend, my brother, I will always miss and love you. I'm grateful for the time we shared together, the miles we walked, and the meals we ate. I will never forget you. Until we meet again—M.C.

And then I read the final text of the evening from Shannon Owen, who held such a special place in both Mitch's heart and mine.

Mitch, tonight when Chadd came over to let us know that you'd gone home, I felt at peace because I know you're with Dad and you are no longer in pain. I felt indescribable sadness for Vickie and Brodie because I know our families are now in the same situation. We will all support and love each other, and we will meet again someday. Thank you for filling Dad's boots and helping us even when you were suffering as well. Love you, Mitch!

Sometime after midnight, alone in the bedroom I'd shared with my husband of twenty-seven years, I picked up my journal and made this entry:

Mitch Speed—you are so loved and will be so missed!
Forever my love,
Vic

Several months earlier, Mitch had given me clear instructions about what I was to do concerning a memorial service. He didn't want a funeral, he didn't want a casket, and he didn't want anyone to wear black. "I want people to celebrate my life, Babe. I want them to eat, drink, be happy, and share their memories."

Though Mitch had made the details of the celebration easy for me, the challenge was finding a venue large enough to hold what we knew would be an abundant crowd. As it turned out, it took two venues to fulfill Mitch's vision. The memorial service would be held Friday, July 27, at The Highlands Christian Fellowship in Palmdale, after which attendees would assemble in the nearby Pioneer Event Center, owned by our friends Marco and Sandra Johnson, for the celebration Mitch had envisioned.

On the one-week anniversary of Mitch's passing, I made this entry in my journal:

July 14, 2018

It's 8:00 p.m., and it will be one week at exactly 9:35 tonight. My heart hurts, and today your absence has become very real. Planning the memorial service is a nice distraction, but it's these quiet evenings that are going to take some getting used to.

God bless my friends; they are my lifeline right now.

I'm not sure how to answer the question, "How are you?" I truly don't know, if I'm being honest with myself.

Brodie is doing well. He is so amazing, just like his dad. To watch him change and grow after losing his father has been such a gift to me.

One week down, and many more to go. What does the new normal look like? Only God knows, and I have to believe Mitch is looking down on us.

Mitch Speed: I am the luckiest girl alive! You showed me love and a life that every girl deserves and wants. I was so blessed to have that with you, and to have you. I will forever say thank you for choosing me. How I'll go on and what my life will look like, I don't know. But I know you always said, "Speed Strong"—so that, I will live by.

Until we meet again, my love,
Vic

The sanctuary was filled to capacity as Brodie and I took our seats for the memorial service, every detail planned according to Mitch's direction. The stage was filled with balloons and flowers, creating a vibrant sense of expectancy, while worship music played in the background.

It was important to our family that we honor everyone in attendance that day; therefore, we reserved a special section for uniformed officers, city and county officials, and upper management of the sheriff's department, including Los Angeles County Sheriff Jim McDonald.

Those who'd known or worked with Mitch throughout the years had often heard him make this statement: "When I die, if the only thing I'm remembered for is being a great cop, then I failed at life." That's why the deputies closest to him dressed in suits that day. They didn't want to remember him only as a law enforcement officer, but as a husband, father, mentor, and a man of God.

I couldn't help but smile when I turned and saw the entire football team from Rosamond High School, Mitch's alma mater where he'd been a volunteer coach and mentor, dressed in their bright red football jerseys. Oh how Mitch would have loved that!

The lights dimmed as a montage of photos streamed across the big screen while the familiar Garth Brooks song "The Dance" filled the sanctuary. Brodie and I looked at each other with a conspiratorial smile when we heard the buzz of hundreds of voices behind us, as one-by-one guests realized it was not Garth Brooks but Mitch Speed doing the vocal.

When John Santero stepped behind the pulpit, he smiled as he introduced Amanda, Shevawn, Jason, and Trey, the worship team Mitch had sung with every Sunday for the past two years. I knew singing without him wouldn't be easy—Mitch was a father figure to the team—but everyone in attendance was moved by the sense of joy and peace these amazing young people ushered into the gathering.

Sheriff Jim McDonald honored Detective Mitch Speed with a eulogy that highlighted his career and his character as a man. But it was the words spoken by our nephews, Christopher Pompa, Justin Neely, and Cody Neely—and a final tribute from our son, Brodie Speed—that painted the most beautiful picture of who Mitch Speed was as an uncle, a mentor, a husband, a father, and the man God had created him to be.

Though I'd purposed to honor Mitch's request to celebrate his life that day, the minutes during which the honor guard folded the American flag and Sheriff McDonald presented it to me and Brodie were emotionally difficult. I'd just taken my place with an exclusive group of Americans who understood the reality of this powerful and familiar statement: *Those who dishonor our flag have never been handed a folded one.*

It was vitally important to Mitch that everyone in attendance that day be given the opportunity to know Jesus as Savior and Lord. John Santero talked about Mitch's faith and then provided the familiar roadmap to salvation, Romans 10:9–10: *If you confess with your mouth the Lord Jesus and believe in your heart that God has raised Him from the dead, you will be saved.* Afterward he extended the invitation for all to attend Mitch's celebration of life: "The Speed family invites everyone to join them at the Pioneer Event Center in an hour for a special celebration that Mitch helped plan. At his direction, the dress is super casual."

As Brodie escorted me out of the building at the conclusion of the memorial service, I experienced such joy in knowing I had honored my husband before the people who meant the most to him. But the day wasn't yet over.

It was literally over one hundred degrees outside that afternoon. The hundreds of people who poured into the Pioneer Event Center were dressed in shorts and flip-flops—a sight Mitch would have loved.

A live DJ provided music as our guests enjoyed food, beer, and sharing memories of Mitch. Brodie spoke again, this time thanking everyone for their love and support, and for honoring his father in such a special way.

But most commented on that day were the unique centerpieces on each table. I'd selected several of my favorite photos of Mitch, printed multiple copies, and then added his signature autograph:

Be blessed,
—*Mitch*—

Every table displayed one of the framed photos, each one decorated with a cross, a fitting epitaph to my husband, Mitch Speed, whom I knew simply as the man behind the badge.

Chapter Five

GOD BROUGHT ME YOU

Tania Owen

Three weeks after my husband was murdered, I was back at work. Though I could have waited longer to return, I was determined that the criminal who'd killed Steve was not going to effectively take us both out. I was also certain my husband would have been the first to tell me to put on my uniform, load Tank in my truck, and return to the station.

The first order of business was to complete the K9 testing Tank and I had begun the day of the murder. On November 18, 2016, I was awarded a certificate that read "Detective Tania Owen and K9 Tank have completed six-hundred hours of instruction in the

Explosive Detection Dog Handlers Course." Tank and I were officially ready for deployment.

I have to say God really blessed me with my K9 partner, though I don't think God brought Tank into my life solely for that purpose. In fact, he played a vital personal role while I muddled through the aftermath of my husband's murder. As a law-enforcement officer trained to keep emotions in check, I never cried in front of others. Rather, I wept for my husband in private. When I surrendered to mourning and allowed my tears to fall, it was Tank who was there with me. He was so in tune with my emotions that he would literally place his paws on my shoulders and hug me. He was my protector—but not my only protector immediately following Steve's murder.

My twenty-two-year-old daughter Shannon was living at home while attending college. Though she had experienced unimaginable trauma—being the first family member to arrive at the hospital and see Steve following the shooting—she was waiting for me at home when I returned from the coroner's office late that night.

The supernatural peace that had descended during the helicopter ride back to Lancaster was still upon me when I laid the bloodstained American flag that had been draped over Steve's body on his pillow and crawled into bed. I knew he was at home with the Lord now, yet his remaining scent on the sheets gave me a comforting sense of being close to him.

As Shannon and Tank slept in the bed with me during those initial nights without Steve, I observed a change come over both of them. Tank became even more in tune with my emotional needs, while Shannon and I seemed to reverse roles. She became what

I can only describe as a *mama bear*—not only for me but also in behalf of our family.

I didn't know it at the time, but Shannon had once promised Steve that should anything ever happen to him, she would be there to take care of me. Through her own pain she stepped into the role of Owen family advocate, never hesitating to deal with the onslaught of public and media attention surrounding the events of October 5, 2016. The pride I feel for my daughter is immeasurable, and I am eternally grateful for the boldness, bravery, and love she demonstrated in the face of dire circumstances.

Just as the Owen family struggled to find stability in the immediate aftermath of Steve's murder, so his law-enforcement brothers and sisters also did at the Lancaster Station. I'd seen the effects of the loss of their sergeant when I attended the debriefing. My speaking to them about Steve Owen, the husband and father, assured them he would want us all to move forward with our lives was a start, but it wasn't enough. After the family and I returned from the Vikings game, I invited Steve's LAN-CAP team—a specialized crime suppression unit—and all the Lancaster Station personnel and their spouses to our home for an outdoor gathering in honor of Steve.

Our house was located on a 2.5-acre piece of property in an unincorporated part of Los Angeles County, with ample room for our horses and other animals. In the center of the huge circular driveway was a grassy area where I set up a tent with plenty of tables for our guests. Several community restaurants donated the food, and one of the Lancaster Station sergeants who made his own beer brought several kegs. He even created a special brew that he named after Steve.

As guests began to arrive that night, the mood was understandably somber, most everyone still in a state of disbelief. Those hit the hardest by the loss were the members of Steve's team, the young men and women he had mentored, trained, and led. Steve's team called him by his nickname "Bullfrog," which had been given to him early in his career.

One of Steve's favorite photos with the team was taken at the 2015 Christmas party, each of the men dressed in a black tuxedo with a red bow tie. That's when his name transitioned from "Bullfrog" to "Frog Father," a take on the 1972 movie *The Godfather*. That's also when I became known to his team as "Mama Frog." Steve and I had been like mom and dad to many of those deputies, and now I wanted to do whatever I could to help ease their pain.

I remember one young man in particular who came up to me and said, "Hey, Mama Frog" and then gave me a hug. I hugged him back, and after a few moments he began to weep. I said, "Don't worry; it's going to be okay."

Still clinging to me, he said, "I'm so sorry I'm crying. I'm supposed to be here comforting you, and instead you are comforting me." I'll never forget that precious moment.

The mood lightened as the night went on and some two to three hundred people came and went. But Steve's team and their spouses remained seated in an area they had staked out for themselves, sharing stories about Steve and their adventures with him. That's when I got an idea.

I walked over to the group and said, "Excuse me for interrupting, but I'd like all of the law-enforcement wives to join me in the house." The first thing I did when we gathered in the family room was ask each woman to write her name and email address on a piece of paper that I passed around the room.

I reminded them that, not only was I a law-enforcement officer, but I was also the *wife* of an officer. I told them that as a law-enforcement wife, I was concerned for their husbands and how they might react to the horrific loss of their sergeant. I explained that rather than express emotion, many men simply shut down because they believe showing emotion is a sign of weakness.

"As wives, we need to be there for our husbands," I said. "During this difficult time you need to be aware of your husband's needs, both emotional and physical. It's important to allow your husbands to release the stress of the issues that are affecting them. Of course, one of the ways they do that is through sex."

I was quite sure I had their attention, so I continued. "Ladies, you still need to be girlfriends to your husbands. Don't wear one of his old tee shirts to bed, wear something sexy—that means no granny panties!" That one piece of advice certainly broke the ice, and we had a good laugh together. But then everyone was engaged and one by one the women shared their personal stories and concerns for their husbands. It was amazing how many women were dealing with either similar or the same issues in their marriages, but knowing they were not alone gave everyone great comfort.

I was pleased to see so many smiling faces as I said goodnight to everyone that evening.

The event on the front lawn was a much-needed, pleasant occasion for all of us. As law-enforcement officers we are accustomed to being in the midst of unhappy occasions. People call 911 when they experience a tragedy. Law enforcement is then dispatched to take charge and handle the situation.

We oftentimes walk into scenes where children are injured or abused, physically or sexually. We routinely answer calls and find someone has been murdered or another tragedy has occurred. We are of course human, but if we were to allow our emotions to take over during these intense times, we wouldn't be able to do what we are called to do: take charge, restore order, and investigate the situation.

That's not to say we are unaffected by what we see but falling apart is *never* an option. After we deal with the immediate need, we have a choice: we can either stuff our emotions deep in our hearts and allow them to fester or learn to deal with those emotions in a healthy manner. All first responders—law enforcement, firefighters, and EMTs—are a particular breed of professionals. As a female cop I always preferred to associate with other cops. I didn't have many female friends, and those I did have were also cops. As a result I had little contact with civilian wives of fellow officers.

Anytime Steve and I would attend a party or social event, I always hung out with him and other guys. He would say, "Hon, why don't you go on over there and talk to the wives? Be with the girls?" My response was always, "No. I'd rather be here with you." Those occasions invariably found me with a group of men.

Perhaps it was my lack of close female relationships that allowed me to ponder my own life and what it would now look like moving forward without Steve. He and I had talked about the two of us doing something to help save marriages, but that opportunity no longer existed. I felt God had a call on my life, but I had no idea what that call was.

I remember a conversation I had with a fellow member of my church, LAPD Sergeant Bobby Vasquez, a man who had a great relationship with God. He said, "Tania, you have a calling to speak to people."

"Me? Why me? Why would God pick me? I don't know the Bible all that well, so how could I possibly talk to others about God?" Sure, Steve and I had discussed helping members of law enforcement who struggled in their marriages, but Steve was the one who knew the Bible, and he could have done the teaching. Not me.

I told Bobby I felt my lack of Bible training was my weakness, but then he opened his Bible and read the story of Gideon. At that time the Midianites were oppressing God's people; therefore, Gideon hid in a winepress to do his work to keep it hidden from his enemies.

> And the Angel of the LORD appeared to him, and said to him, "The LORD is with you, you mighty man of valor!"
>
> Gideon said to Him, "O my lord, if the LORD is with us, why then has this happened to us? And where are all His miracles which our fathers told us about, saying, 'Did not the LORD bring us up from Egypt?' But now the LORD has forsaken us and delivered us into the hands of the Midianites."

Then the LORD turned to him and said, "Go in this might of yours, and you shall save Israel from the hand of the Midianites. Have I not sent you?" (Judges 6:12–14).

Of course, Gideon obeyed the Lord, and as a result the Bible says, *Thus Midian was subdued before the children of Israel ... And the country was quiet for forty years in the days of Gideon* (Judges 8:28). God transformed Gideon from a fearful young man hiding in a winepress to a mighty man of valor.

From then on Bobby referred to me as Gideon. When I saw him, he would say, "Okay, Gideon, what are we doing today?" Honestly, I had no idea what I was doing for the Lord, but I was open to His instructions. A couple of people suggested I write a book or take up public speaking, but I certainly wasn't prepared for such endeavors. And quite frankly, I didn't have the time.

My sister, Maria Laglaive, was in the final stage of her two-year battle with ovarian cancer. The disease had spread to other organs in her body, requiring her hospitalization. Each week, on my days off, I would make the five-hour drive from Lancaster to Salinas, California, where I was allowed to stay with her in her hospital room.

Though she never complained, Maria was in constant pain, oftentimes crying out in her sleep. During the night I was her advocate with the hospital staff and during the day I was her companion and comforter, doing what I could to cheer her in the face of the greatest trial of her life.

One day she looked at me and said, "Tania, I'm scared."

I moved closer to her and looked directly into her eyes. "What are you scared about?"

"I don't know where I'm going when I die."

That's all I needed to hear. Immediately I began to witness to her about Jesus, and how I'd accepted Him as my Lord and Savior. I told her how God had healed my marriage, how He'd given me unimaginable peace just months earlier when Steve had been murdered. And then I opened my Bible to Romans 10:9–10 and read these words: *If you confess with your mouth the Lord Jesus and believe in your heart that God raised Him from the dead, you will be saved. For with the heart one believes unto righteousness, and with the mouth confession is made unto salvation.*

My sister accepted Jesus as her Lord and Savior that day and then, on February 24, 2017, she went home to be with Him. The peace that had first descended on me the day Steve was murdered again enveloped me. Maria was no longer in pain, she was totally healed and set free. Within four months' time I'd lost both my husband and sister. Though Maria and Steve were no longer part of my present, I had peace in the assurance they most certainly awaited me in my future.

I was at home on March 5, 2017, my first birthday following Steve's murder five months earlier, when Mitch Speed and fellow deputy Dave Kessee came to my door with a beautiful green plant in hand. "Hey, Tania! Vickie, Dave, and I remembered it's your birthday, and we wanted you to have something that will bring you years of pleasure," Mitch said. "Just don't forget to water it," he added with a smile. I thanked him and invited them in for a cup of coffee at the kitchen table.

Mitch and Vickie, as well as several other deputies, had been attending my church, The Road Church of the Antelope Valley, since I'd invited members of the Lancaster Station to join me when I spoke at Steve's debriefing. Because of my work schedule, I wasn't always able to be at church each Sunday, so I appreciated the opportunity to visit with Mitch. He was battling cancer, yet he looked well and maintained a positive outlook of faith. Our conversation was light and uplifting, though he did say in passing, "Tania, I know you'll take care of Vickie for me."

He went on to say, "But your birthday isn't the only reason we came to see you. I'm going to start a Tuesday-night Bible study at our home for members of law enforcement, and I'd like you to come. Of course we'll study the Bible, but there will be plenty of time for discussion. I plan to send a group text, but I wanted to invite you in person and let you know your children are also welcome."

The previous October I'd felt so blessed and humbled that Mitch had accepted our invitation to sing at Steve's funeral, and now he was opening his home to us. Mitch Speed had made an unspoken blue-line commitment to take care of the Owen family, and now that is just what he was doing.

Our entire family felt drawn to Mitch and the comfort he gave us. Tyler lived out of town and was unable to join the Bible study, but Chadd, Shannon, and her fiancé, Parker, and I faithfully attended each week. Being with my law-enforcement family in an atmosphere of love and faith was a gift from God.

With each passing week I could see the impact cancer had on Mitch's body, yet his spirit remained strong. I couldn't help but think of the comment he'd made on my birthday: "I know you'll take care of Vickie for me." But what did that look like?

Though I saw Vickie each week in her home, we didn't have what either of us would have described as a strong friendship. The thought of approaching her on a personal level while she and Mitch were in the fight of their lives actually caused me anxiety. I remember praying, "Lord, I need your help. Please show me what to do." The answer to my prayer came quickly.

I'd just received an insurance settlement following Steve's death, which got me to thinking about Mitch and Vickie's finances. He was no longer working, so I reasoned that perhaps I could be a blessing to them financially. When I attended church the following Sunday, June 17, 2017, I noticed Vickie was there alone. Throughout the service I sensed God's gentle nudge that it was time to approach her.

I waited until Vickie exited the building and walked toward her vehicle. I hurried to come alongside her and said, "Hey Vickie, do you have a minute?"

She smiled and said, "Sure Tania. It's good to see you."

I took a deep breath. "I need to ask you something and I don't want to offend you, but how are you and Mitch doing financially? I want to write you a check." There, I'd said it.

"Oh, Tania, I'm so grateful for your offer, but I have to say no thank you. By God's grace Mitch and I are actually doing well."

I thought that might be the end of the conversation, but we continued talking as the peaceful presence of God enveloped us.

I was relieved she wasn't upset by my offer, for I knew I needed to befriend her, not offend her.

For the next three hours the palpable presence of God remained with us as we openly laid out our lives to each other. I was amazed at the ease I felt in speaking to Vickie, who was, after all, a civilian wife. And then she said, "I want to tell you something I've never told anyone else."

I sensed the significance of the moment, and instinctively went into my professional listening mode. As a detective I knew the importance of remaining focused, engaged, and quiet when someone trusted me enough to be open and honest.

Vickie said, "Early one morning in June of 2016, I was sitting alone on my patio having a cup of coffee. Mitch had just been diagnosed, and I was trying to wrap my head around the seriousness of his condition and how we were going to face the virtual death sentence pronounced by the doctors."

She paused a moment, I nodded, and then she continued. "That's when I had what I can only describe as a vision. As I looked at the beautiful blue sky above me, I saw God's hands open up—they were huge. And then I heard Him say, 'Vickie, I'm going to prepare you to live this life alone.' That was the end of the vision; it was the most beautiful image I've ever seen. I knew then that Mitch was going to die, yet I felt God's perfect peace. And it is with me still."

I was so honored Vickie would confide in me such a personal account, and I felt myself actually connecting with her for the first time.

I certainly understood what she meant about God's peace, so I told her of the peace I'd experienced at the time of Steve's murder.

I also recalled the Bible verse that had come to my mind that day: *Be anxious for nothing, but in everything by prayer and supplication, with thanksgiving, let your requests be made known to God; and the peace of God, which surpasses all understanding, will guard your hearts and minds through Jesus Christ* (Philippians 4:6–7).

I told Vickie of my sense that God had a calling on my life, something He wanted me to do, but I had no idea what it was. "I know I'm supposed to do something, but just not right now."

Vickie said, "Wouldn't it be cool if you and I could do something together one day? But I agree the time is not now—not while Mitch is still battling."

Things changed between Vickie and me that day. We started talking more each week at Bible study, and afterward the kids and I would always stay a while after the others left. Chadd and Shannon would talk with Mitch while Vickie and I strengthened our bond. I started visiting Mitch on a regular basis—sometimes I'd go by myself, other times with one or two deputies. I was beginning to feel as if I were his big sister.

When Mitch's health took a turn in the spring of 2018, I remember going to the Speed home with two other officers and making dinner for Mitch and Vickie. Each time I was in their home, I felt the bond of our relationship growing. That's why I felt conflicted about attending the annual National Police Week in Washington, DC, in May where tens of thousands of law-enforcement officers from around to the world gather to honor those who have paid the ultimate price.

A number of members of the LAPD planned to honor the fallen of 2017 by riding their bicycles from Hollywood, California, to

Washington, DC, to participate in the week's activities. I was going to accompany them in my motorhome to provide support. From start to finish the trip would take one month.

The seed of friendship that had been sown when Vickie and I talked in the church parking lot was coming forth. I told her of my plans to attend Police Week, but I added that if anything happened to Mitch, I would immediately catch a plane back to California. When I saw Mitch and Vickie at church the Sunday prior to my leaving, he didn't look well. I was concerned to the point that I wondered if this would be the last time I would see him. If so, I wasn't going to leave anything unsaid. I gave him a kiss on the cheek, hugged him, and told him I loved him.

As it turned out, I did see him again. By the time I returned from Police Week, Mitch was in a wheelchair, unable to use his legs. My two close friends, LAPD Sergeants Bobby Vasquez and Miguel Mejia, and I brought dinner to Mitch and Vickie at their home, but our time together that evening was bittersweet. Mitch was unable to stay awake, and Miguel and Bobby had to carry him to bed. Bobby and Miguel were not only brothers in blue, but they had also become very close to Mitch as brothers in Christ.

After that evening Vickie and I remained in contact via text. The Speed family was no longer receiving visitors, and I wanted to respect their decision. Then, on the night of July 7, 2018, I received a text from Vickie that simply said, "Mitch went home."

I immediately felt I needed to be with her, so I reached out to her, and she agreed I should come. Several other people were already there with Vickie and Brodie when I arrived, and after she and I talked for a few minutes, I asked if I could see Mitch.

Vickie said yes and allowed me to go to his bedside. I felt the peace of God as I gazed tenderly at the man who had been my friend, my brother, and a comforter to my children and me during the darkest days of our lives. I thought how like Jesus he was, this godly man who had lived his life to serve others. I could think of no better way to honor Mitch than to rub his feet—the feet that had for years carried the gospel of Jesus Christ everywhere he went. As I ministered to his body, I said my goodbyes to my friend, finishing with the words, "God bless you, Mitch."

I then sat with Vickie until the coroner's vehicle arrived. The presence of God was tangible on both her and Brodie as they thanked Him that their husband and father was now healed, pain free, and at home with his Lord and Savior. As Mitch's body was borne from his home to the waiting vehicle, dozens of deputies standing at attention lined both sides of the sidewalk.

Whereas I had chosen to honor my husband by escorting his body to the coroner's office, Vickie chose to honor Mitch as he had requested by remaining at home with family and friends, praying and allowing the Comforter—the Holy Spirit—to envelop them with the peace of God.

Honor is a standard of conduct we each demonstrate in our own unique way. I was blessed that Vickie allowed me to stand with the Speed family in such a special and intimate time of honoring the husband and father who had touched so many lives.

On Friday, July 27, I rose and put on my dress uniform in preparation to attend Mitch's memorial service. Though many of the deputies who'd worked with Mitch wore civilian suits and clothing, wearing my uniform was my way of honoring the amazing man I considered my brother in uniform.

It blessed me to see Vickie surrounded by so many family members that day. My relationship with her had deepened in recent months, yet I chose to remain in the background during the service and give her space. My eyes were often on my friend as the beautiful service unfolded. Perhaps the most significant moment for all was when the recorded song "The Dance" played and we realized it was actually Mitch's voice doing the vocal. I smiled as I recalled Mitch singing at Steve's funeral and how I'd then looked at him and smiled.

When I did connect with Vickie briefly following the service, someone snapped a photo of the two of us, leaning into each other and smiling as she told me how much peace my being there gave her. It is a photo we both treasure today.

My friend and fellow church member, Bobby Vasquez, was a great source of comfort to me as I grappled with processing the loss of our dear friend Mitch Speed. Bobby often texted Bible verses that never failed to bring peace and offer hope. More importantly, Bobby was there for me as I prepared to face the initial court hearing for the man accused of Steve's murder.

I'd spoken to Steve's mother, Millie, about the upcoming case and let her know I wanted the death penalty. I went on to explain that I wasn't angry about what had happened and had no feelings of animosity for the suspect, but she called me out on what I said.

"Tania, you may say one thing, but I've known you long enough to recognize the anger you keep so well hidden. You know what Jesus says about the matter: *"And whenever you stand praying, if you have anything against anyone, forgive him, that your Father in heaven may also forgive you your trespasses"* (Mark 11:25).

Truth be told, I was rebellious. At that moment I felt as if I were being *forced* to forgive and I wanted none of it. "Millie, I'm not there yet, and I don't know if I ever will be."

The next time I saw Bobby I told him about my conversation with Millie, how she'd identified my anger though I'd insisted I was fine, and how I'd not been receptive to the idea of forgiveness. Not surprisingly, Bobby agreed with Millie and proceeded to put me in my place.

Following that initial conversation about forgiveness, Bobby and I continued to talk about the matter, and he always prayed with me, gently stepping me toward obedience to what I knew was God's will.

One day he said, "Tania, if you died, and when you got to heaven you saw Steve waiting for you—with the suspect standing next to him—would you then forgive the man?"

"Yes," I said without hesitation (surprising even myself with my answer).

"Why would you forgive him?"

"Obviously, if he's in heaven with my husband then he asked God to forgive him, which means he is now my brother."

That conversation really opened my heart to forgiveness. I realized that forgiving the suspect didn't mean the trauma he'd caused my family and I was insignificant, nor did it mean he should escape the consequences for the murder he'd committed. I had always said that I refused to allow him to take out *both* Steve and I; by forgiving the suspect I was actually removing the chains of unforgiveness that would have kept *me* bound for as long as I allowed them to do so.

Isaiah 52:1–2 paints a beautiful visual image of the act of forgiveness: *Awake, awake! Put on your strength, O Zion; put on your beautiful garments ... Shake yourself from the dust, arise ... Loose yourself from the bonds of your neck, O captive daughter of Zion!*

By the time I went to the first court hearing—two years after Steve's murder—I'd truly forgiven the suspect. As Millie, the kids, and I waited in the hallway outside the courtroom with our attorney, I asked him if the suspect's family was among the many people waiting to enter the courtroom. When he said yes, I asked him where they were. He pointed down the hallway where I saw two women, his mother and sister, speaking to two attorneys.

I immediately went directly to the women and said, "Excuse me, I don't mean to interrupt, but I want to introduce myself. My name is Tania Owen. I'm Sergeant Steve Owen's wife, and I want you to know I don't want you to feel intimidated by my presence or my family's presence.

"I have nothing against you because I feel you are victims just like I am. You didn't pull the trigger and you are not responsible for what happened to my husband. Like I said, I just wanted to introduce myself." Both women thanked me and reached out to shake my hand, but instead I gave each one a hug before walking away.

Because I had *chosen* to obey God, I was able to see those two women through the lens of forgiveness, which enabled me to approach them. Later in the day, Millie hugged the mother and every member of our family spoke to those two precious women whose lives had also been irrevocably altered by the horrific events of October 5, 2016.

Vickie Speed and I saw each other mostly at church for the remainder of 2018 as she sorted through the practical matters of life and transitioned into a new season.

But then in January of 2019, we took the first step together into a new chapter of our lives.

The Lancaster Station announced plans to compete in the annual Baker to Vegas race that year in honor of Mitch Speed, and they invited Vickie to attend as their guest. I was thrilled when Vickie told me of her plans to go and then was surprised when she added, "Tania, I want you and Shannon to come with me."

So in March Vickie, Shannon, and I made the four-hour drive to Las Vegas where we spent four wonderful days and three nights with each other and thousands of members of our law-enforcement family. What the three of us learned from attending that event together was just how much we enjoyed being with each other.

Once back in Lancaster, Vickie and I had dinner weekly, sat together in church each Sunday, and often dropped by each other's homes to visit. God was knitting our hearts together as only He could, and one shared desire of our hearts was that we do something to honor our husbands, though we didn't yet know what that looked like.

I'd honored Steve by attending Police Week each year and had even invited Mitch to join me in 2017, though he hadn't been able to attend. Police Week 2019 was coming up in May, and Shannon and I planned to attend. But then I thought, *I should invite Vickie to go with me*—and so I did.

Being at Police Week meant a lot to Vickie that year. The three of us went to the National Law Enforcement Museum, attended a candlelight vigil in honor of fallen officers, and saw Steve's name on one of the two curving marble walls at the National Law Enforcement Officers Memorial. It was a solemn moment for Vickie, Shannon, and me as we experienced the respect shown for the men and women who'd lost their lives in service to others. We remained at the memorial wall for the afternoon to meet and greet the arriving bicycle riders on the Police Unity Tour, who had just completed a three-day ride to honor the fallen. Our close friend LAPD Sergeant Miguel Mejia had ridden in honor of Sergeant Steve Owen and Detective Mitch Speed.

We also had fun while we were there. We loved going to Kelly's Irish Times, a pub synonymous with Police Week. There, along with scores of other Police Week attendees, we enjoyed great camaraderie, music, and beverage while listening to Host Sergeant John Krupinsky. We traded stories about Steve and Mitch with other blue-line families and joined in the famous midnight toast honoring all fallen officers, followed by live bagpipes.

We met two incredible law enforcement officers at Kelly's, whom we now consider to be great friends. They have given true meaning to blue line family.

Vickie and I returned to Lancaster with the realization that, not only had we honored our husbands that week, we'd become family. As we navigated through our lives without our husbands, we found that, in addition to leaning on God, we could lean on each other. Ours was an easy relationship.

One beautiful October day in 2019, as Vickie and I headed home on the freeway, we were again talking about our mutual desire to honor our husbands and do something to help law-enforcement marriages—a matter for which we still had no direction. I remember Vickie looking at me and saying, "What are we going to do? I'm an accountant who runs numbers, and you shoot people."

We were laughing really hard, and then simultaneously we said, "We need to write a book!" We joked around about what kind of book to write and laughingly said we could do a law-enforcement devotional or a book titled *How to Survive Your Marriage*. Though the conversation was almost silly, something seemed right with the idea of writing a book.

We'd both retired in 2018, so it wasn't like we didn't have the time to put together a book. We just didn't know how. What's more, we didn't know what we would say. The more we talked about the matter over the coming days, the more convinced we were that the Lord was leading us to write a book based on our personal experiences, the loss of our husbands, and—most importantly—how God had healed our marriages.

In January of 2020 God laid it on Vickie's heart to reach out to one of our community leaders, a respected businessman who had known both Steve and Mitch. He and his wife agreed to meet with us and then listened attentively as we shared our ideas for writing a book and also for establishing a foundation in honor of our husbands to help law-enforcement marriages. The couple assured us that our ideas were solid and doable, and then they spoke wonderful words of encouragement to us. They connected us with several professionals who could advise and help us as we moved forward in faith.

We also shared our vision with our pastors, John Santero and Jason Grundy, who prayed for us and offered to help any way they could. But Vickie and I knew it was up to us to take the first steps, and for us that meant being totally transparent about our lives and marriages—both with each other and with our future readers. The proverbial rubber was about to meet the road.

Part Two

THE GOOD, THE BAD, AND THE REALLY BAD

Therefore be imitators of God as dear children. And walk in love, as Christ also has loved us and given Himself for us, an offering and a sacrifice to God for a sweet-smelling aroma. For you were once darkness, but now you are light in the Lord. Walk as children of light.

EPHESIANS 5:1-2, 8

Chapter Six

LIFE IN THE ANTELOPE VALLEY

Vickie Speed

Though California's Antelope Valley is some thirteen hundred miles from Kansas where *The Wizard of Oz*'s Dorothy and her dog, Toto, were launched by a tornado into their amazing adventure, as a child I was always taken aback by the movie's poppy-field scene. To me, it looked just like home.

Having lived virtually all of my life in the Antelope Valley, a high desert area in northern Los Angeles County, I was accustomed each spring to the explosion of color cascading down the rolling hills for miles on end. California poppies bloom nowhere more brilliantly or profusely than in our valley.

More than half a million people call the valley their home. These residents live primarily in the cities of Palmdale, Quartz Hill, Rosamond, Lake Elizabeth, Leona Valley, and my hometown of Lancaster.

When my parents divorced shortly after my birth, my mother moved with my older brother and sister and me to Lancaster because she thought it was a great place to raise kids. Mom remarried when I was eighteen months old, and though my real dad was always part of my life, it was my step-dad who actually raised me. I always referred to him as Dad.

My memories of growing up are all good. We were a simple, middle-class family who went through both good times and hard times. We lived in a small home where my mom and dad were extremely loving parents, though Dad's military background set the tone for our very strict upbringing. Typical of most children, I thought the rules were too strict; however, as an adult I now understand the value of what we learned. We all want to raise good children, strong enough to stand on their own two feet.

Two significant events occurred in our home when I was twelve years old. The first occurred when I was looking for something in our local newspaper one day and noticed a full-page ad. The headline read "I Found It" and listed an 800 number a person could call to come to know Christ. So I called the number and spoke to a nice lady who said she was sending someone to my house. I wasn't sure how my parents would take the news, but it turned out they were okay with it. When several people from our local Baptist church arrived and met with our family, they opened their Bibles to Romans 10:9: *If you confess with your mouth the Lord Jesus and believe in your heart that God raised Him from the dead, you will be saved.* Our family accepted Christ together that day, and we soon made First Baptist Church of Lancaster our church home

The other significant event that year was when Dad suffered a heart attack and had triple bypass surgery. I didn't realize it at the time, but that was the beginning of his being sick for the next six years. During that time he had several more heart attacks, and when I was in high school, his heart had weakened to the point he was forced to retire from Lockheed.

Both my brother and sister had graduated from high school and were no longer living at home, so it was just my parents and I. Mom worked in the social services department at Mira Loma hospital, and I could see how tough it was on Dad to watch her have to get up and go to work each day and come home tired each night. I always admired his concern for her.

During my senior year in high school, Dad's health took a turn for the worse, which took him in and out of the hospital. In February the decision was made that I would step away from school and stay home to care for my dad. I knew this was something my mom especially needed me to do, and I honestly didn't have a problem with it. We were a family, and in my mind, this was the kind of thing you did for your family.

Dad passed away in April 1983 after suffering a massive heart attack at home. Though I was now eighteen, his death had a traumatic impact on me. Little did I know God was preparing me for my future.

Only two months later Mom's dad died, and she fell completely apart. All of a sudden it was as if I'd become the parent and she the child. As I watched Mom surrender to hopelessness and sorrow, I remember telling myself, "I will always be a strong woman."

I finished my senior year at summer school and then went to work for the Department of Defense. I learned a lot during my time there, but after two years of dealing with the stifling structure of government work, I decided to get a job in private industry. I was offered an entry-level position as a payroll clerk for a construction company and soon discovered I loved working with numbers. Within four years I'd worked my way up to office manager.

Life was good for me. I was twenty-one years old and single, had a steady job, and was living on my own. My best friend, Valerie, was a hair stylist who worked at a nearby walk-in salon, and on weekends I'd often hang out there while she took care of her clients. I was there one day, sitting in a chair as I flipped through a magazine, when several guys about my age came in together to get haircuts. I couldn't take my eyes off one in particular: a tall, good-looking man wearing a cowboy hat, boots, and well-fitting jeans. When I asked Valerie to introduce me she said, "I don't know him, Vickie; besides, he's not my client. If you want to meet him, why don't you introduce yourself?"

There was no way I was going to approach a man I didn't know, so I just sat there like a schoolgirl and watched him from behind my magazine. I was sad when he and his friends left. But then, a couple of months later, I was in the salon one Saturday when he came in. Just as before, I asked Valerie to introduce us. Again she said no and told me to go talk to him. I couldn't do it, so for the second time, without even knowing his name, I watched him walk out the door once his haircut was finished.

Several weeks later I was with some girlfriends having drinks and listening to a band at a popular bar where twenty-somethings came from throughout the Antelope Valley to hang out and have fun. The good-looking guy I'd seen twice at the salon was also there, and we ended up meeting that night. Surrounded by my girlfriends and emboldened by a couple of beers, I actually stole his cowboy hat and told him that if he wanted it back, he could call me and take me out.

We went to dinner the very next night, and what I discovered was that Mitch Speed—the handsome cowboy in the well-fitting jeans—was an absolutely perfect gentleman. I was particularly touched with his kindness, and remember thinking, *There's no way there's a guy like this out there.*

I'd recently come out of a long-term relationship and, despite my attraction to Mitch, I wasn't sure I was ready to start dating. So about a week later, I told him, "I need you to know I do not want a boyfriend," to which he responded, "Thank God, Vickie. I don't want a girlfriend either, so we're gonna be good as friends." I remember thinking, *Well, that wasn't really the response I was looking for, but it's okay.*

As it turned out, Mitch and I became the *best* of friends. He was in the construction business, which meant he worked out of town a lot. But when he was home, we often hung out, spending our time getting to know each another.

Mitch told me he'd been born to a single woman who'd given him up for adoption to his parents, James and Barbara Speed, who already had one adopted son, Bill. When Mitch was in the second grade, James and Barbara divorced. Though James neither paid child support nor was in the boys' lives for a number of years, Barbara was determined to raise two strong men. To that end she moved to Rosamond, where she put herself through college while working at Edwards Air Force Base. She purchased her first home, which—with absolute faith in God—she ruled with a firm hand. Though Mitch and Bill were raised in a modest environment, they appreciated everything they had. Barbara taught her boys they could accomplish nothing significant in life without putting God first.

One thing I discovered was that Mitch's demeanor never changed; he remained the perfect gentleman always, and I never saw him lose control of his temper. I considered myself a very lucky girl for having met this too-good-to-be-true, six-foot-three handsome guy who wore a cowboy hat.

I remember thinking one day as we were driving down the freeway, *Wow, he's marriage material. He's the guy you want to take home to meet your mom.* My next thought was, *What am I thinking? I don't want to get married—get that out of your head!* But over time what began as a friendship grew into love, and ten months after we'd met, Mitch asked me to marry him. Of course I said yes, so together we began to plan our wedding and a future based on our shared Christian faith and values.

Mitch worked at his father's topsoil, excavating, and grading company, and the plan was that we would one day buy the company. We'd even talked to his father about it. We had a two-year plan that started with purchasing the business, followed by buying our first home and then having a baby. Beyond that initial plan, our marriage dreams stretched ahead of us like yards of velvet ribbon on an exquisitely gift-wrapped package.

The following year on August 24, 1991, we married. Ours was a traditional church wedding with about 250 in attendance, and I remember thinking, *We're the lucky couple—our life is going to be perfect.*

Six weeks later I was pregnant. Mitch and I often laughed and said we were still doing laundry from our honeymoon when we figured out we were pregnant.

Though we hadn't planned to start our family so soon, Mitch and I were both twenty-six years old and excited about becoming parents. When I was five months pregnant, Mitch and his dad had a huge blowout, and Mitch walked out; the company subsequently went under. I remember thinking, *But we were going to buy the company and our life was going to be perfect in our huge house with the white picket fence.* In reality we lived in a little apartment, I was pregnant, and my husband was unemployed.

Mitch's non-existent employment status had the potential to create some tension in our marriage, but it didn't. My husband was the hardest working man I'd ever met; he was a strong man, raised to take care of his family, and in my heart I knew he would do so. We didn't know what lay ahead, but we had two mothers who prayed for us and assured us God had a plan for our lives. We'd had our own plans, but God laughed, and now we were on a different journey. Although Mitch and I had both been raised in Christian homes and wanted God in our marriage, we hadn't located a church home as a married couple; so at that time we were neither attending church nor growing in our faith.

After a couple of months, Mitch went to work for the federal government as a heavy-equipment operator at Edwards Air Force Base. It certainly wasn't his dream job, but it enabled him to take care of his family.

James Brodie Speed was born on July 20, 1992, and as his parents, we couldn't have loved him more. Brodie's birth was especially meaningful to Mitch because he'd been adopted at birth. To him, having a son who was his own flesh and blood was a gift from God. A month later we celebrated our first wedding anniversary with a beautiful, romantic dinner by candlelight—while I simultaneously nursed our baby.

When we celebrated Brodie's second birthday, Mitch was still working at the base and I was managing the construction office. What I didn't know at the time was how unhappy Mitch was with his job, and needless to say, his unhappiness couldn't help but spill over into our home life. We were about to buy our first home, yet our plan of raising a family felt more like we were going through the motions rather than living our dream.

But then Mitch made a significant connection with Kevin, one of the airmen at the base who also was a songwriter from Oklahoma. While in high school Mitch had often written poetry, stories, and songs. Now he began collaborating with Kevin and a few other military guys, and the creativity that had lain dormant all those years began to come to life. I watched Mitch thrive as he dove into his passion for writing, which soon spawned the birth of a country band, Mitch Speed and Mendin' Fences. I was pleased my husband had something to do for fun, but things changed when the band's first CD, also named *Mendin' Fences*, was an immediate hit.

Soon, Mitch, Kevin, and the others were playing an increasing number of weekend gigs and were even invited to open for some really big names. I loved watching the band play for these events—it was so cool and exciting. In addition to his songwriting abilities, Mitch had an amazing voice and entertained the idea of moving to Nashville to see if he had what it took to really make it in the music industry. But I knew I didn't want that kind of life, so the moving-to-Nashville option was quickly taken off the table.

Mitch continued to work at the base Monday through Friday, while the weekend gigs increased steadily over the next few years. Though I enjoyed going with him when I could, most of the time I stayed home with Brodie, who had just entered grade school. The gigs generally ended around 2:00 a.m., and it wasn't unusual for the band to enjoy a beer before going home. Mitch was usually home by 3:00 a.m., but over time 3:00 a.m. became 6:00 a.m.

As confident and strong as Mitch was, he found it easier to sing if he'd had a few beers before getting on stage. This comfort became a regular weekend ritual with one beer becoming two or three, and then more. Of course, with his newfound celebrity status came a whole group of available female fans who didn't care that he was married and had a family. Thankfully I was married to a man who took his vows seriously; however, I wasn't a dumb woman—I knew full well things could happen when people were out drinking.

I remember one Saturday night in particular. Mitch had just come home and gotten into bed with me when the phone rang. When I answered, a female asked to speak to Mitch. As a good wife does, I handed the phone to him and said, "It's a girl for you. You might want to let her know that it was your wife who answered," and then I rolled over and went back to sleep.

When we discussed the matter the next morning, Mitch apologized. Though I wasn't angry, I didn't share my thoughts about how his weekend life conflicted with the life I wanted and the way I wanted to raise our son. I wasn't sure this life was what I'd signed up for, but I trusted Mitch.

Mitch had grown up in the small town of Rosamond, where there wasn't much to do. Teens often gathered at R Mountain (Rosamond Mountain), where they drank beer and did stupid things. For Mitch, growing up in a small town with very little to do, drinking was a weekend normal. His drinking had slowed down after we married, but as the band grew more successful and popular, the weekend drinking became a bigger part of his life. I didn't mind at first; after all, the extra income had afforded us some luxuries beyond what our salaries would otherwise have provided. But after a couple more years of Mitch being gone Friday and Saturday nights and then sleeping all day Sunday, I reached a breaking point.

We had poured thousands of dollars into the CD and band equipment to give Mitch the best opportunity of being signed by a record label. But despite his exceptional talent, no offers had materialized. I missed spending time with my husband, and Brodie needed his father, so after having a conversation with Mitch about the importance of his being there for us, he agreed to adjust his schedule. Things went well for a while, but then around the fifth year of the band's existence, we hit a wall.

We owned a boat, and I'd planned to take it one weekend to a nearby lake to enjoy time with family and friends. It was to be an adult trip, and Mitch had agreed to stay home and spend time with Brodie that day. The plan was that, following his previous night's gig, he would be home at 3:30 a.m. to hook up the boat for me before going to bed so that I could leave the house at 5:00 a.m. When I got up to get everything loaded, Mitch wasn't home and the boat wasn't hooked up. He wasn't home by five o'clock, and he wasn't home by six o'clock either. Needless to say, Mama wasn't too happy about the situation.

When Mitch pulled in the driveway at 6:15 a.m., I could tell he'd had a lot to drink. He hooked up the boat, but there was no way I was going to leave Brodie with him in that condition, so I packed him up and loaded him into the vehicle. Before I climbed in myself, I said, "Mitch, it's time for you to make a decision. I've supported your dream to be a singer, and I'm proud of what you've accomplished with the band over these past years. But this is no longer a lifestyle I want. It's not enough for me, and our son needs a father present in his life. I'll never ask you to give up your music or anything you love, but you need to figure out how you're going to balance it with a healthy home life. I'm not going to do this anymore."

Brodie cried all the way to the lake. To a little boy, I was now the bad guy for not letting him stay with his dad. He had looked forward to spending the day with his father, and as the only child on the boat that day, his presence altered the dynamic for everyone who thought we were to have an adult excursion. When I got home around 8:00 p.m., I was more emotional than angry when Mitch came out to meet me. His demeanor couldn't have been more polar opposite than when I'd last seen him. "Let me help you, Vic," he said and then backed the boat into place and unhooked it.

Mitch told me he'd been thinking all day about what I'd said and he realized how important his family was to him—too important to allow the band to continue taking so much of his time and focus. The band had several gigs scheduled over the upcoming weeks; however, Mitch was true to his word. He laid off the drinking and came home immediately after each engagement.

I could sense Mitch was struggling. I knew he'd never been happy with his job, but something was definitely going on with my husband—I just wasn't sure what it was. The matter became clear in a matter of weeks when his friend and bandmate, Gregg Cox, was diagnosed with leukemia. In the years they'd performed together, Gregg had become one of Mitch's mentors. Unbeknownst to me, Mitch had been talking to Gregg about his goals and dreams. Gregg had encouraged Mitch to find his life's passion and pursue it.

Though Gregg wasn't allowed to have visitors, I went with Mitch to the ICU to visit his family. As we left the hospital, Mitch told me that in a special moment they'd recently shared together, Gregg had said, "Hey, Buddy, remember to follow your dream."

Two days after we visited his family in the hospital, Gregg was gone; his passing marked a turning point for both Mitch and our marriage. It was the day my husband made the decision that the band stopped and the drinking stopped. He needed to be present as a husband and a father, and he needed to follow his dream for his life—whatever that might be.

Around the Speed household a new sense of peace settled, allowing me to experience a level of contentment I'd never known. But that peace was momentarily shaken one day when Mitch appeared at my office, something he *never* did, and said, "Vic, I need to tell you something." My first thought was that something had happened to Brodie, but Mitch assured me all was well and then said, "Did I ever tell you that when I was twenty-one years old, I wanted to apply to the sheriff's department?" I told him no, and then he continued. "Well, someone told me I'd never make it and that I shouldn't bother applying, so I didn't."

I remember thinking, *You came all the way over here to my office, and this is what you wanted to tell me?* I had no idea where this conversation was going, but Mitch had more to say. "You know, the loss of Gregg really made an impact on me. He'd been talking to me for quite some time about following my dream, which I thought was a singing career, but I see now that was wrong. I don't know how to tell you this, but I just applied for the sheriff's department today, and I passed."

My mouth literally dropped open. "You *what*?"

"There's more. I have to be back in the morning, and I have to buy a suit. I need you to go with me to pick one out."

And with that, the Speed family took its first step toward becoming a law enforcement family. In reality Mitch was walking away from a steady job with no guarantee he'd make it through the academy, but he had two things going for him: One, we agreed this was the best decision for him and for us. Two, I had complete faith in my husband. I knew failure was never an option for Mitch; he could do this.

Our biggest hurdle was the fact that the arduous, twenty-four-week course at the Los Angeles County Sheriff's Department Training Academy would be conducted in Whittier, California, some ninety miles from our home. This meant Mitch would need to move there.

The next six months were challenging, especially for Brodie who desperately missed having his father at home. But every Friday after I finished work, we'd make the drive to Whittier and spend the weekend together. Though the time of separation was tough, I understood law enforcement was truly a calling on my husband's life. When Mitch graduated in 2003, Brodie and I couldn't have been happier for him in light of all he'd accomplished in moving toward his dream.

I don't know what I'd expected; however, adjusting to a life in law enforcement was a positive experience for the Speed household. For the first few years, Mitch worked the jails as all new deputies do. His schedule allowed him time at home with Brodie and me, and overtime was minimal. Brodie was proud his dad was a cop—a fact that earned Brodie the respect of his peers. I was truly proud of my husband and the life he provided for us; most of all I loved that he was now happy in his career.

Besides, there's something to seeing your man in uniform that is—let's face it—sexy!

Chapter Seven

THE REST OF THE JOURNEY

Vickie Speed

The Speed family had adapted to its new normal: Mitch was building his career, I was working in a job I loved, and Brodie was an active junior-high student. We had a roof over our heads, food on the table, family toys, and time to take vacations. Life was really good.

The next step in Mitch's career was to go through patrol training to become a patrol deputy. Though he didn't have to relocate as he did with his initial training, the rigorous six-month program demanded his full focus. I wanted to do all I could to ensure his success, so I assumed all responsibility for running our home, paying bills, handling household and vehicle repairs, and coordinating Brodie's sports schedule.

On top of that, my new job in the Motocross industry required that I travel on weekends. I couldn't have imagined a more fun and fulfilling job; however, with Mitch's six-month commitment to training, we'd become accustomed to seeing each other mostly in passing. I wondered, *Have we really become the married couple just going through the proverbial motions?* Thankfully the situation was temporary—or so I thought.

In reality, Mitch's completion of training and then his going to work patrol were eye-openers for me. I had no idea the extent of the job requirements, in particular the crazy shifts and long hours. But seeing Mitch absolutely thrive in that environment helped me make a decision: despite his lengthy hours being tough on me, I was okay with his new schedule. I'd continue taking care of things at home because I knew I was a strong woman, able to face and overcome any circumstances that came my way.

Mitch continued to advance in his career, moving to the specialized Robbery Suppression Team. He especially loved the team's sergeant and the deputies he worked with, and considered it a high honor to be included. I was excited for my husband because I knew how much this job advancement meant to him. But that's when things at home really changed.

The long hours became even longer as his team was required to be available 24/7. When the phone rang—whether at 9:00 p.m. or 3:00 a.m.—with a burglary call that required response, Mitch had to go. Clearly, crime didn't stop; therefore, neither did Mitch Speed. The more he progressed in his career, the more I felt as if I were a single mom.

The one shared love in our life was Brodie, now a freshman in high school and a straight-A student, despite Mom and Dad's revolving-door lifestyle. I was preparing some promotional material for the upcoming Motocross weekend one day when I got a call from a woman in the administrative office at Brodie's school. She told me Brodie was currently in the principal's office and asked if I could come immediately to speak with the principal.

When I arrived, Principal Devin Thomas met with me privately. He asked how Brodie was doing at home and if we followed his schoolwork online. Well, of course Brodie was doing fine at home; however, neither Mitch nor I were involved with his studies. That's when Mr. Thomas informed me that Brodie was actually failing two classes and had made a D in another. Seems that at school he also had an attitude issue and an ego issue. I thanked Mr. Thomas for his concern and for letting me know. Then I assured him Brodie's father and I would take immediate action at home.

Mitch and I were both shocked by what we'd learned. How could this be? Brodie was a good kid who'd always been a good student; what had changed? As we took a step back to assess the situation, we realized neither Mitch nor I had considered the shock Brodie experienced when moving from junior high to high school. He was used to being around kids no older than himself, and then he was thrust into an environment where he was surrounded by seventeen- and eighteen-year-olds. We'd assumed things were good with Brodie as they'd always been.

As Brodie's parents we had to take an honest assessment of our situation and the fact that our respective jobs were actually creating an atmosphere of instability in our home, for which our son was suffering. We had to do something and do it fast; in other words, one of us had to give up something. The decision wasn't difficult for me, though it *was* disappointing. Mitch had a thriving career that would always enable him to take care of our family while fulfilling his dream. Though my job in Motocross was fun and satisfying, in essence it was just a job. As a mom I was unwilling to sacrifice my son's wellbeing. So I quit—and I never resented Mitch for that decision.

For the remainder of the school year, my job was Brodie. Mitch and I had both been raised by parents who believed to spare the rod was to spoil the child. We agreed Brodie would no longer be left alone at home; one of us would always be there (plus my mom lived nearby and was available if needed). My new routine involved driving Brodie to school each morning and picking him up in the afternoon. Then we went straight home, where I helped him with homework. I watched him like a hawk, and my efforts were rewarded when Brodie finished his freshman year with a great GPA.

With Brodie back on track to balance his academic life with sports for the remainder of his high school years, I was ready to go back to work. I returned to the construction industry, accepting a position in accounting and project management for a family-owned company just seven minutes from our home. Though not as thrilling as Motocross, I found odd fulfillment through managing big public works projects that dealt with the construction of water systems, schools, prisons, and court houses.

While I never resented my decision to quit my previous job, the time I spent at home with Brodie made me realize I was indeed harboring resentment—for Mitch's job. Mitch had often said that

THE REST OF THE JOURNEY

as Christians the order of our priorities should be as follows: God, spouse, kids, and work. Why then did I feel as if I were fourth in his list of priorities? My solution for the situation was to bury my feelings and be the best mom I could be. My life consisted of work, watching Brodie's high-school sports events, and frequent "retail therapy excursions" for my own emotional wellbeing, courtesy of the credit cards I carried in my purse.

Brodie graduated from high school in 2010 and announced to us he wanted to attend college and do something big with his life. Mitch and I couldn't have been any prouder of him. The summer passed in what seemed a blink of the eye, and then it was time for Brodie to go to college. He'd chosen to start his college career at Cuesta College in San Louis Obispo, a junior college known for its excellent education program. His plan was to get his general education and also play basketball while at Cuesta.

My emotions were all over the charts the day Mitch and I dropped Brodie off at school and then climbed into our vehicle for the three-hour drive back to Lancaster. On the one hand, I was excited my son was in college and had his whole life before him. I remember thinking, *At last Mitch and I will have the house to ourselves—with no piles of laundry to do and no shoes lying around everywhere. It doesn't get any better than this.* On the other hand, I had tears in my eyes as I realized Brodie was taking his first steps into adulthood. It was no secret Mitch felt much the same. The drive home proved emotional for both of us.

What we didn't realize was that day marked a breaking point for Mitch and me, though it didn't really come to light for several months. We still lived in the same house and held the same jobs. But without Brodie at home, we didn't know each other, didn't know what to talk about, and no longer had anything in common. Sadly, we didn't love each other as we once had; actually, I'm not sure we even liked each other at that point. We'd existed in the same house for eighteen years, being parents but never taking the time to nurture our marriage. We were in trouble.

Mitch had never been one to lose his temper, and we'd never fought as some couples do. When we finally sat down together to address the matter of our marriage, my resentment of his job spilled out. Throughout our marriage Mitch and I had both worked to provide for our family; however, in my opinion his career had become his first love. I remember saying, "Mitch, I just want you to love me as much as you love your career." I knew he really did love me more than his career, yet it didn't feel that way.

Truth be told, I'd played a part in creating the stalemate in our marriage, because I'd never told him how I felt. What I really wanted was for my husband to be as excited to see me at the end of his shift as he was to go to work each day.

During our talk that day, we spoke openly about our feelings and the fact that for years we'd been going through the motions of being a family, merely existing in our lifeless marriage. I can say with certainty I had no feelings for my husband when I looked at him and said, "I don't think I want to do this anymore. Is there anything left? If so, where do we go from here?"

The one piece of remaining common ground between us was our belief that the vows we'd made when we'd married were forever, which meant we had no choice but to stick it out together. I'd like to say we jumped immediately into action and took steps to save our marriage, but that didn't happen. We had absolutely no idea how to fix things, yet we knew we were not going to separate.

Living under the same roof was a chore as we came and went, each with little regard for the other. That's when Mitch came up with an idea: "Vic, how about we take a first step and agree not to do anything to make each other angry? If we leave our personal issues at the front door, maybe we can find a way to be friends again and move forward."

It seemed a good place to start, and though there wasn't any depth to our relationship, it worked. We'd taken our first step.

With our similar Christian upbringings, Mitch and I both knew that to succeed in marriage, God had to be front and center. Rather, we had both been *taught* the concept of God's being front and center—but neither of us had ever *learned* it, for neither of us had ever *lived* it. At best, our church attendance had been hit-and-miss throughout our twenty-three years of marriage. We soon realized our sporadic record revealed the truth about our spiritual priorities: we had never put God first.

One evening Mitch came home and said, "Vic, I've made a decision for me. I don't know where you're at, but I know I need to work on me; I need to fix *me*. So I'm going back to church and I'm going to become the man God created me to be."

All I mistakenly heard was that *I* had to go to church, and the very thought made me cringe. I'm now ashamed to say that I didn't want to go to church, but I just wasn't interested. I told him, "You know what, Mitch, I really support you in this, and I think it's great that you're going back to church. But I'm not ready to go with you."

Sure enough, Mitch started going back to church by himself each Sunday, and I was fine with that. But after a while it began to bother me. While I didn't want to go to church, at the same time it irritated me he would go without me. Not the most rational position on the matter.

Mitch didn't pester me about going to church with him; instead, he simply reaffirmed his own reason for going: "I don't want to fix you, Vic. I want God to fix me, to change me. I feel that if He changes me, I can be a better husband and father." In reality, I was watching my husband change right before my eyes. Mitch had never been a bad husband; he'd never spoken to me or treated me in a way that shattered my soul. But now I could see in him something new—softness, kindness, and a different kind of love as he continued to say, "I want God to change me."

I could see Mitch meant what he said, and I knew God needed to change me too. I'd spent so much time in my marriage wanting to change Mitch, thinking his transformation would solve all our problems, that I'd fought the idea of going to church. But then I changed my mind and decided to go. I thought if Mitch and I didn't make it, I could at least say I tried. Looking back, that definitely wasn't my proudest moment as a wife.

I remember the Saturday night I told Mitch I would go to church with him the following day. He didn't react, just nodded his head and said okay. Over the following few months, we were still the "hit-and-miss" church attendance couple: Mitch was the hit, and I was the miss. But Mitch never chided me, just remained consistent in attending, standing firm on his upbringing. His mother had instilled in him the belief God had to be first in the home, and I could see that Mitch was truly fighting for our marriage and our family. He was determined God would be front and center in our home and in our lives.

Mitch had every reason *not* to become a great husband and father. Having been adopted at birth by parents who soon afterward divorced and having had a father who was an absent parent throughout his childhood, Mitch had been raised by a single mother caring for two boys on her own. Mitch also should have died when, at age ten, he had an aneurysm burst. But Mitch had never let his circumstances define him, and he wasn't about to now; he made up his mind to become the man God created him to be.

I'd like to say that our journey to restoration and wholeness was a smooth one, but it wasn't. I remember one particularly difficult exchange we had during those early months of church attendance. Though Mitch and I never argued with each other, we most certainly had disagreements. During one of these disagreements, I poked him a little too hard, and he said, "Do you know what your problem is?"

My response was defiant. "No—what?"

"The problem is that you want me to be Prince Charming. I don't know how to tell you this, but you ain't Cinderella!"

That line was probably one of the most painful things my husband ever said to me, yet his words hit their mark. Sadly, what Mitch said is true of so many women. We *are* oftentimes looking for that tall, dark, handsome Prince Charming, first to date and then to marry. We get married, and the first thing we want to do is attempt to change our Prince Charmings, yet we are not willing to change ourselves.

Because I knew I was absolutely guilty, that painful exchange became a defining moment for me. I needed to stop picking apart everything my husband said and did, and spotlighting every fault and mistake. I needed to go to God and say, "What do I need to do to become a better me? To become a better wife and mother?" And that's just what I did. The first thing I had to do in working on myself was truly leave Mitch to God. My priority was to become the best wife and mother I could be. It wasn't my place to see that Mitch became the best husband and father possible.

I never discussed my decision with Mitch, but once we'd both made the commitment to work on ourselves, putting God front and center in our marriage, things immediately began to change.

One of the things I learned from God was that He wanted me to honor my husband. I'd had the mistaken idea that doing so would make me weak, just the opposite of the strong, independent woman I was raised to be, which was one of the reasons Mitch had chosen me to be his wife. But God assured me if I would simply honor Mitch and focus on being the wife I was supposed to be, He would work on Mitch and take care of everything else. And that's exactly what happened.

With God now the center of our marriage, Mitch and I were actually able to sit down together and talk as friends. In so doing, it quickly became apparent we really did love each other, we were in our marriage forever, and it was worth fighting for. One of the passages of Scripture that meant a lot to me was Ecclesiastes 4:9–12 (NIV):

Two are better than one, because they have a good return for their labor: If either one of them falls down, one can help the other up. But pity anyone who falls and has no one to help them up. Also, if two lie down together, they will keep warm. But how can one keep warm alone? Though one may be overpowered, two can defend themselves. And a cord of three strands is not quickly broken.

To me, those words painted a beautiful picture of my marriage to Mitch and the significance of our making God the third strand in our cord. Though Mitch and I had been married for nearly twenty years, we were falling in love in a new and exciting way. I honestly didn't remember having ever loved Mitch that deeply, and I was grateful for all God was doing in our lives.

As I continued to work on my own issues, allowing God to transform me into the woman I was created to be, the point came where I needed to take a stand and face the personal demons I'd carried for so long. I had to be honest with God, and I had to be honest with my husband. If Mitch and I were going to have the kind of marriage we wanted, there could be no secrets and no lies.

For years I'd continued to bear a deep resentment for Mitch's job. I resented the hours it kept him away from his family, but mostly I resented his commitment to the job and the joy it brought him. We'd vowed to remain together for better or worse, and in my mind the job was the "better" part for Mitch while home life was the "worse."

I also needed to come clean with Mitch about the amount of debt we carried. The responsibility for our family's finances had initially fallen to me when Mitch entered law enforcement, and it had remained there since. For years I'd used my credit cards for purchases that never really seemed to fill the void in my life I attributed to Mitch's work-related absence from our home.

The first thing I did was lay it all out before God and ask His forgiveness for my attitude toward Mitch's job, for my irresponsible actions with finances, and for keeping everything from my husband. The Bible says, *If we confess our sins, He is faithful and just to forgive us our sins and to cleanse us from all unrighteousness* (1 John 1:9). Going to God was the easy part; I still had to tell Mitch.

I have to say that God's grace was with both Mitch and me throughout that difficult conversation. Mitch listened without interruption or judgment as I apologized for the resentment I'd carried for so long concerning his job. Then, to my utter surprise, he didn't become upset when I told him about the six-figure credit-card debt—but he made it abundantly clear, as of that very moment, things were going to be different. He told me the debt was *our* debt and we would take care of it together. The most painful part of the lesson was that he meant it when he said, "No more new cars, toys, dinners out, clothes shopping, and *no new shoes*."

It would take us four-and-a-half years of working our butts off to wipe out the debt, but God's timing is always perfect in everything. We paid the final bill in October 2017, nine months before Mitch passed. He had such peace in knowing he was leaving this earth with his family being financially whole and my having learned how never to be in debt again.

The conversation I had with Mitch about our debt was difficult; however, I immediately felt the freedom that came from bringing everything out of the darkness and into the light that day. But we weren't done yet.

I knew going into the conversation that in essence I would need to put some tape over my mouth long enough to allow Mitch to speak and that I would need to really listen to what he had to say. In the time I'd been seeking God about making me a better wife and mother, I'd come to understand that I needed to allow my husband to talk to me about his job so that he didn't bottle things up inside. Being a first responder is tough—mentally, physically, and emotionally. It's a 24/7 lifestyle that can't be turned off with a switch.

When Mitch spoke, his words were measured, his tone respectful, and his demeanor filled with love. "Vic, my home is my safe haven. I'm not a perfect husband, and I know I don't always do a lot to help you around the house, but I'm so often physically and emotionally spent when I come home that all I want to do is shut down. At those times the thing I dread more than a honey-do list is the thought of you being angry with me because you see a husband who doesn't help. All I see is a man who needs to clear his head and recharge."

———

It takes a strong person to be married to a first responder. With God now firmly established first in our lives and marriage, I knew without a doubt I was strong enough to take on life in a way that truly made my husband's life easier. The best way I could honor my husband was to find the great qualities God had placed in him and focus on those qualities. For me it meant I needed to put on my big-girl panties and handle business when he couldn't.

With God's help I learned to respect Mitch's job. Though he loved his work in law enforcement, I knew the reason he was doing it was to provide a blessed life for his family. Because Mitch loved his job, when I chose to love it too something shifted in our marriage. Our son was in college, and it was time to change some things as we entered a new season in our lives.

Before Mitch walked out the door at the beginning of each new work week, we prayed together, asking God to bless Mitch's week, our home, and our marriage.

We also established each Thursday night as "dinner together night." Unless Mitch was doing a warrant, we would meet someplace at 5:00 p.m. sharp for whatever amount of time he was available. Sometimes it was only thirty minutes, sometimes it was an hour or more. We'd talk about nothing in particular, or we'd talk about everything: our son, church, or Mitch's job, which I no longer resented. He would usually go back to work after dinner, sometimes not getting home until 3:00 a.m., but I was fine with it.

Mitch was happy again, and I was happy for him. He'd progressed from the burglary team to robbery and then to assault. In addition to these advancements, he received departmental awards on a regular basis—proof positive of the great job he was doing.

When Mitch left the house each morning, it was never without our exchanging an "I love you" and a kiss. We had an agreement about his job and the situations he could possibly get into: If he didn't answer my call, I would know he was tied up with something. If I received a text that said *I love you*, I'd know it was code for

Something is going down. In such a case I'd always stop to pray for him but then get back to my daily life without fear because I trusted my husband, the training he'd received, and God.

Mitch always told me that if anything out of the ordinary happened, I'd be the first to know. I took comfort in his thoughtfulness. If he wasn't home by 2:00 a.m., he would text to let me know he was still working and what time he thought he'd be home. I learned I needed *trust* operating in my marriage but, even more so, I needed *faith* operating—the faith of knowing beyond a shadow of doubt that every day when my husband walked out the door, I could be certain he would come home to his family at the end of his shift.

As we took time to focus on our lives and where we wanted to be in twenty years, we had to ask some hard questions. Where are we in our marriage? What are we doing to fight for it? Are we living to please the world or please God?

Mitch had to ask himself some questions about his life and job. Am I living to make a mark with a badge, a gun, and a uniform, or do I want to make a mark for God? This amazing job will come to an end one day, but what will I have given to my home life and my family?

Our new goal was to grow old together, and we were excited about the future. I was particularly blessed to watch Mitch develop and grow in his spiritual life. He was brave as he stepped out onto the cliff where he told the world, "I'm not afraid to become the great man God created me to be." Mitch openly shared the Word of God, openly prayed, openly believed. He told everyone how much he loved his wife and family. He read the Bible and every other book he could find about faith to fuel his heart, mind, and soul. He wasn't afraid of what the world thought of him.

None of these factors changed when Mitch was diagnosed with cancer. If anything, he was more determined than ever to touch the lives of others with the love of God. Each time Mitch sang in church, standing with his arms in the air and his fists clenched, I always cried—not because he was sick, but rather, because he was a picture to the world of a man God loved completely, in spite of his brokenness.

Mitch was dying, but nothing in this world was going to slow him down. And nothing in this world, not even death, could separate either of us from the love of God—the God who took the shattered pieces of our marriage and gave us something beautiful in return.

"Because the Lord *has anointed Me ... to give them beauty for ashes, the oil of joy for mourning, the garment of praise for the spirit of heaviness; that they may be called trees of righteousness, the planting of the* Lord, *that He may be glorified."*

ISAIAH 61:1, 3

Chapter Eight

FROM EL SALVADOR TO CALIFORNIA TO LAW ENFORCEMENT

Tania Owen

Situated between Guatemala and Honduras on Central America's Pacific Coast, El Salvador is the smallest of the isthmus's seven countries. Its economy is mostly agricultural and its religion predominantly Catholic. This is the nation where I was born.

I was the youngest of four siblings. My sister was eighteen years older than I, so my constant companions were my two brothers, with whom I enjoyed endless hours of playing marbles and pretending we were soldiers. Our parents worked, so we spent a lot of time with our grandmother, who often took us to visit her brother in a nearby town. He lived in an adobe house that had neither electricity nor an indoor bathroom. We slept on a mud-type bed and always went to sleep when the sun went down.

Everything we ate came from the land. If we wanted eggs, we gathered them from our chickens. If we wanted milk, we got it fresh from the cow. I remember how much I always enjoyed a fresh glass of warm milk. We cooked outdoors on a fire pit covered with a metal grate. If we wanted to make tortillas, we would simply go pick some corn. Then we would shuck it, remove the kernels from the ear, and make the masa.

If we wanted to take a bath, we went to the river, where we could also wash our clothes by adding some soap and using a smooth, clean rock as a scrubber. By today's American standards my early years were very humble; however, I didn't know any different way to live.

To me life was always great and beautiful—despite the fact I was born with clubfeet, a condition where both feet are rotated inward and downward. Though the condition does not affect the overall health of a baby, living in a third-world country in 1965 meant my parents didn't have access to the same medical technology available in the US. For the first year of my life, I wore casts on my legs to straighten them. When the casts came off, I was fitted with braces so that I could learn to walk. I remember my dad working with me for hours on end to help me recover and move into regular shoes, though they still had metal inserts to ensure my feet remained straight.

Most of the kids I played with were the boys on my street. Having been raised with two brothers, I was a pretty feisty little girl, so anytime the boys would try to get the best of me, I'd kick them with the metal tip of my boot. I learned to hold my own with those boys, many of whom were afraid of me.

When I was nine years old, my family immigrated to the United States where we made our home in Santa Monica, California. The transition was difficult for me. Leaving my grandmother and the familiarity of the only life I'd known was traumatic, but even more traumatic were the things that happened in our home. I was now old enough to understand the domestic abuse my mother had suffered for years at the hands of my father.

On the one hand I recognized my father's possessiveness of my mother, and on the other hand, his complete lack of respect for women. I also learned to recognize the situations when Mom's words or actions would inevitably lead to a beating. During those times, I would hide in a closet, cover my ears, and pray to God, asking Him to make it stop. It was then I told myself I would never allow a man to treat me the way my father treated my mother and I would never marry a Hispanic man. Conversely, my father was very loving to me. I was his little girl, which was really conflicting for me. I resented my father for treating my mother the way he did, yet loved him for being a great dad to me.

By the time I turned fourteen—with my sister married, my eldest brother in the Marine Corps, and my dad no longer living with us—my other older brother and I were the only family members still residing with Mom. The three of us shared a two-bedroom apartment.

As a single parent, my mother struggled to feed us and pay the rent; however, she refused to ask for assistance. She would say,

"We're going to do this on our own. If we have to eat rice and beans so that we can fight on our own, then that's what we're going to do."

Because I admired my mother so much for her resolve to make ends meet without any help from the outside, at age fourteen I started working to help our household. Going to work at such an early age didn't seem a bit strange to me. After all, that's what young people often did in my culture. Eventually I worked two jobs while going to school. Half the money I earned went to help with bills, and the other half was put into savings for college.

At that time I thought I wanted to become a doctor—that is, until I went to my school's Career Day, saw a classmate standing at one of the booths, and asked about the police uniform he was wearing. He explained he was part of the Santa Monica Police Department Explorer Program. I learned that Law Enforcement Exploring was a youth-oriented, hands-on, career-discovery program that gives young men and women the opportunity to learn about law enforcement through actual experience and training.

I had grown up playing soldiers with my brothers. As a young woman on the verge of adulthood, I'd come to appreciate the discipline and structure the Marine Corps afforded my eldest brother. Both military features remained powerful draws for me throughout my years at Santa Monica College, after which I applied with the Santa Monica Police Department. I was sworn in as an officer in 1986 on my twenty-first birthday.

In late 1987 I transferred to the Los Angeles County Sheriff's Department and started working the jails. By the time I was twenty-three, my life experience and law enforcement training had given me an unwavering conviction in my ability to do my job and carry out my duties, oftentimes in the face of some pretty scary people and situations. I was a confident and resolute deputy, yet on the inside I was continually wrestling with a dark and exhausting emotion—fear. I'm not talking about the kind of fear one experiences in the midst of a dangerous situation. I speak of a fear that nagged me day and night like a cloaked intruder—the fear of the unknown, specifically not knowing what would happen to me when I died.

I'd been raised Catholic but had developed quite a rebellious attitude toward the basic tenets of the Church. I didn't understand why I had to confess my sins to the priest or say a certain number of Hail Marys or Our Fathers for my sins to be forgiven by God. Where was *that* in the Bible?

Some of the deputies who worked the jails with me were Christians, and they invited me to join them for a Bible study. For the first time in my life, I heard the gospel of Jesus Christ presented in its purest form, direct from the pages of the Bible, without the filter of religion: *If you confess with your mouth the Lord Jesus and believe in your heart that God has raised Him from the dead, you will be saved* (Romans 10:9). The moment I accepted Jesus Christ as my Savior and Lord, the fear left, for then I knew *exactly* where I was going when I died.

Having been assigned to the LA County Antelope Valley Station in 1990, I was working patrol as a deputy sheriff. At that time the Antelope Valley was a melting pot of demographics. Though there were areas with elevated crime rates, a growing number of people were moving to the AV to escape the crime that ran rampant in other areas of Los Angeles County. Parents fled LA to keep their kids out of the gangs; however, little did they know their children brought the gang life with them to the Antelope Valley.

I remember arriving at the station for my shift one day and noticing a deputy I'd never seen before talking to one of our AV Station deputies. Something about the new deputy's demeanor made me think he had a chip on his shoulder. I shook off the feeling, walked over to him, and introduced myself. His name was Steve Owen, and he'd just been transferred from the Lynwood Sheriff's Station in Los Angeles.

The Lynwood Station was known for virtually continuous action due to the high crime rate in the area. Located in the heart of Los Angeles County, the station regularly sent its deputies out in response to shootings, gangs, narcotics activity, and carjackings—all of which became more active when the sun went down. Our station wasn't nearly as busy as Lynwood's, and I wondered how Deputy Owen would adjust to a different pace and different demographics. It didn't take long for me to form an opinion. Based on the questions he asked, it seemed clear Owen didn't want to be here, and I don't think it an exaggeration to say he was arrogant. I left the encounter with a bad taste in my mouth.

I was not happy to learn I'd been assigned to work three shifts with Owen during the upcoming two-month period. The first time we worked together in a patrol car, we had minimal discussion with each other. We were there to respond to calls, and that's exactly what we did—strictly business. The same was true of the second time we worked together; however, I'll never forget a particular incident that occurred the third time we worked together.

We were in a remote area of the Antelope Valley when we stopped a young man. Both of us got out of the car to talk to him, and Owen took the lead. From the beginning of our encounter, the young man was very respectful to Owen; however, Deputy Owen's attitude was really negative. I didn't say a word throughout the exchange, and when we got back in the car, I was pretty frustrated with my partner.

I turned to him and said, "You know, you're the kind of deputy that makes people not like us." He obviously didn't know what I meant by that statement. He didn't say a word, so I continued. "If anything had happened to you and you'd gone down, based on the way you just treated that guy, do you think he would have helped you or just turned his back and walked away?"

Owen remained silent, so I kept talking. "I understand when someone treats us with disrespect or refuses to cooperate, we need to take certain steps. But there was no need to treat that individual the way you did. As deputies we have to deal with all kinds of people, from children to city officials to criminals, and we have no right to treat any of them badly."

We didn't speak another word to each other that day. I knew Owen had a wife and two young boys, and I remember thinking, *I wonder if he's this charming at home with his family?* Thankfully, I wouldn't have the opportunity to find out. When we ended our shift that day it would be several years before Owen and I would work together again.

In 1992 my personal life took a positive turn when I married. It was a blessing to be married to someone also in law enforcement who understood the demands of the job. The following year I became pregnant, but I didn't let my condition slow me down. I was in great physical shape, I loved my work, and I had my doctor's approval to work as long as I wanted to.

On March 13, 1994, I finished my shift at midnight and then went home and crawled into bed. Four hours later I had my first labor pain, and nine hours later I delivered the most beautiful baby girl ever, whom we named Shannon Nicole. I hadn't known my heart could be so full of love, and I thanked God for the blessing of this child He'd brought into our lives.

After I'd been on maternity leave for six weeks, it was time to go back to chasing bad guys and protecting the community I was sworn to serve. My husband and I worked different shifts, so we alternated caring for Shannon. If we had to be gone at the same time, Shannon's nana (my incredible next-door neighbor, Dana Tussey) was there to take loving care of her.

When Shannon was one year old, I was one of several deputies chosen to go work our gang unit, a specialized group of deputies who target gang issues. After each of us had initially worked several months with a specific detective, our sergeant told us we would be assigned new partners for the next four months. My partner was to be Steve Owen, already an investigator with the gang unit. I remember thinking, *Not if I have anything to say about it.*

I went to my sergeant and said, "Sir, if it's okay I'd rather not work with Owen. I don't like him, so could you assign me to a different partner?"

He promptly said, "You don't have a choice. Too bad, so sad—that's who you're working with."

Unbeknownst to me, Owen had also gone to the sergeant and told him he didn't want to work with me. Not surprisingly, he'd received the same response as I had.

So there we were, together again after four years. Clearly nothing had changed between us. We took up right where we'd left off, neither of us talking to the other unless it pertained to the task at hand.

I quickly realized Owen was experienced in working with gangs, so I made the decision to adapt to the situation and to continue functioning as a professional. We often found ourselves in dangerous situations, whether arresting gang members or trying to help people, and we slowly began to form a bond of trust.

At some point we laid down our mutual animosity and started talking to each other. When we actually began to discuss our police work, I learned Owen was a pretty phenomenal street cop. He had an in-depth knowledge of the law where it pertained to making arrests, and knew everything there was to know about gangs, narcotics, weapons—you name it. As I watched him build rapport with gang members, I realized what I'd initially misinterpreted as Owen's arrogance was actually his confidence in his abilities.

I saw this confidence regularly demonstrated in conversations he had with individuals as we transported them to jail. First, he took the time to explain *why* we'd arrested them. He told them the arrest was actually an opportunity to turn their lives around, if they chose to do so. He said he was willing to help them; however, if they chose not to accept his help, the reality was they would likely end up dead. Many of those young people accepted his offer, and Deputy

Owen was true to his word. On his own time, he checked on them and their families. As a result, he became a father figure to many.

One thing I particularly admired about my partner was that he never shortchanged the station on the time he put in on his shifts. Whether ten hours or twelve, he always gave 100 percent. For instance, if our shift ended at midnight and we'd brought in a bad guy and finished booking him at 11:40 p.m., Owen would be back in the car and on the street for the twenty remaining minutes of the shift. If it turned out we arrested someone in that period of time, it wasn't unusual to stay until after 2:00 or 3:00 a.m. doing paperwork. I never saw him take advantage of any of his time at work.

During those months I learned a lot from Deputy Owen, and I soon realized that what he'd brought to the table was making *me* a better street cop. We got into a lot of really good pursuits and worked some exciting cases together. In the course of our working together, we formed a professional bond and a cordial friendship. And then our sergeant announced that it was time to split the teams. Again, both Owen and I went to our sergeant, but this time we each requested to stay together. And again, our requests were denied.

Prior to going our separate ways, I thanked Deputy Owen for his professionalism and all I'd learned from working with him. Then I added a personal comment: "Owen, I want you to know something."

"What's that?" he said.

"I see right through you. You may act like a grizzly bear while you're on duty, but I know you're just a big teddy bear."

I didn't wait for him to respond; I simply turned and walked away.

I was back on patrol the following year and would occasionally see Deputy Owen out in the field when we had lunch or took a coffee break with our respective partners. Though we didn't see each other often, our friendship remained cordial and comfortable.

The one thing in my life that *wasn't* comfortable was my home life. My husband and I had married in the belief that our mutual foundation of being in law enforcement would keep us on firm ground, but we had been wrong. As it turned out, we had little in common, and without a shared faith in God (I was a Christian; he wasn't), our relationship unraveled and ultimately ended in divorce.

The transition to single motherhood was a challenge, but I faced it head-on and did what I had to do to make shared custody with Shannon's father work. I was determined to make my daughter's life as normal as possible, and I wanted her to know both of her parents loved her despite our own differences.

In July of the following year, I attended a one-day law enforcement training seminar along with a number of other deputies from the Antelope Valley Station. When I arrived at the meeting location, I was pleased to run into Deputy Owen, whom I hadn't seen for some time. Following the morning session, a group of us went to lunch together, which gave Owen and me time to play catch-up. That's when I learned he and his wife had divorced the year prior to my divorce, and he was still having a difficult time adjusting to sharing custody of his two young boys, Chadd and Tyler.

His pain was so real and raw, I stayed and talked to him while the others returned to the seminar. Owen talked to me openly about his emotional pain, his concern for his boys, and his faith.

That afternoon, for the first time, we actually connected as friends, as brother and sister in Christ.

Throughout the coming weeks and months, we had numerous conversations about our lives, in which I learned a lot about Steve Owen. He was born in Encino, California, in June of 1963, and his brother, David, followed two years later. His parents, John and Millie Owen, were blue-collar workers. Steve's dad worked for the Department of Water and Power; his mother was the administrative assistant at Granada Hills Baptist Elementary School.

Steve remembered his early years as happy ones that included family going on camping trips, riding dirt bikes, and taking trips to various lakes where the boys learned to water ski. His favorite lake was Arizona's Lake Powell.

The Owen home was a Christian home. Steve accepted Jesus at a young age and dedicated himself to reading the Bible so that he could develop his own relationship with Christ. Growing up, he attended Christian schools and always loved sports. As one of the captains of the football team at Los Angeles Baptist High School, he played on both the offensive and defensive lines. He also participated in track and field, specifically shotput.

After graduating from high school, Steve attended junior college at College of the Canyons in Valencia and worked part time in a local supermarket as a night-shift manager. Anytime a shoplifting incident occurred, he would inevitably turn from manager to loss-prevention agent, which meant he assisted in the capture of the thieves. Even back then he was compelled to stand for what was right. He could tolerate neither stealing nor being a victim.

FROM EL SALVADOR TO CALIFORNIA TO LAW ENFORCEMENT

One night an incident occurred that changed the course of Steve's life when he gave chase to several armed robbers who had used fake guns to get the cashier to turn over the store's money. As Steve was closing the gap between the robbers and himself, one of the men turned around, aimed the fake gun at Steve, and fired. When Steve heard the rounds whizz past his head, followed by the sound of breaking glass behind him, he realized the guns weren't fake. That's when he ended the foot chase.

But a day or two later, he spoke to a friend who had recently graduated from the sheriff's training academy. His friend encouraged him to become a law enforcement officer, and Steve thought, *If I'm going to get shot at, I might as well get paid for it.* He graduated from the Los Angeles County Sheriff's Department Training Academy in 1987 and, after working a short time in the county jails, was assigned to work patrol in South Central Los Angeles, where chasing down bad guys and being shot at was a familiar experience.

The more I got to know Steve Owen the man, the more I got to know who he was as a person—and I liked what I saw. My view of Steve Owen, the deputy I had so disliked in the beginning, had changed completely and I was starting to have feelings for him. I couldn't believe it.

We began to date, and after several months those dates included our children: his boys, Chadd and Tyler, and my daughter, Shannon. The kids got along well, and the more we spent time together the more I could see what a loving father Steve was to his boys and the kindness and love he showed my daughter. As a single mother, it was important that whomever I was with would be good to my daughter first, and me second. Steve's steadfast and loving interaction with Shannon is what convinced me he was the one.

After dating for a year, Steve asked me to marry him. While I wanted someone in my life who would love me and be a kind and loving stepfather to my daughter, it was Steve's relationship with Christ that was the determining factor in my accepting his proposal. The Bible warns *Do not be unequally yoked together with unbelievers* (2 Corinthians 6:14). I had ignored that warning when I entered into my previous marriage, but I knew Steve and I were equally yoked in our belief in Christ and our love for Him. We wanted to bring up our children knowing the Lord and having their own relationships with Him.

Steve and I decided to wait a year before marrying. We'd both been through difficult divorces and knew the success rate for second marriages wasn't good. We wanted to take the time to know with certainty this marriage was what we really wanted and that blending our families was right for our children.

God was important in our relationship from the beginning. Steve and I prayed together as a couple, regularly attended church with the children, and always prayed as a family when we had dinner together.

As our relationship deepened, so did our conversations. Neither Steve nor I wanted to go through another divorce, so we agreed that the word *divorce* would never be uttered in our marriage. However, we were realistic enough to know that even the best of marriages experience problems. I made Steve promise me that when—not if—we faced problems in our marriage, we would go to counseling and fight together for our marriage.

FROM EL SALVADOR TO CALIFORNIA TO LAW ENFORCEMENT

Law enforcement marriages have their own unique challenges, such as enduring lengthy periods of time away from one's home and family. Because *both* Steve and I were in law enforcement, we would experience the additional challenges of working different shifts and having different days off. Having once been partners (though we didn't like each other at the time), we were well aware of the bond that can form between two people when they depend on each other for safety and emotional support. If a marriage is fractured, it's easy for one or both spouses to form emotional ties with members of the opposite sex. What begins as an innocent conversation can quickly become an affair.

I told Steve that our relationship was no longer about only two people, it included five people. I said, "I've opened up my heart to love your boys, so if our marriage were to fail, I would lose three people whom I love. Unless your intentions are to stay with me forever, let's not get married." We made the commitment to each other that counseling would be our *only* option in the face of any situation whose resolution seemed impossible.

On October 23, 1999, Steve and I were married in a beautiful outdoor ceremony in Lancaster, attended by about 150 of our closest friends and officiated by our dear friend and Lancaster Station Chaplain Billy Pricer. I wore an off-white, floor-length wedding gown, and Steve looked so handsome in his black tuxedo. Steve's brother, David, was his best man, and my best friend, Kelly, was my maid of honor.

It was important to Steve and me that our children be included in the ceremony; after all, five of us were coming together that day, not just two. I was so touched when Steve got down on one knee and made his vows to five-year-old Shannon. He said, "Shannon, I promise I will be a good dad to you—an involved and caring dad who will always be there for you. I promise to pick you up if you ever fall, and I promise to always love you." With each promise Steve made, Shannon nodded her head in affirmation as if she clearly understood what he'd told her. Steve concluded by presenting her with a gold ring, which he placed on her right ring finger.

Next I got down on one knee before the boys and said, "Chadd and Tyler, I promise to love you as much as if I'd brought you into the world. I will always be there for you, and I will help you anytime you need me." When I finished placing a ring on each of their fingers, there wasn't a dry eye in the house. All three kids were so incredibly happy they were included in the wedding.

Following the ceremony, we went to another location to celebrate throughout what turned out to be a great evening. When it was time to cut the wedding cake, I took advantage of my new husband's cool demeanor as I smeared his handsome face with cake frosting. He laughed and took it in stride, and then I softly told him he'd better not do the same to me—which he didn't.

The next morning Steve and I were off to Hawaii for our honeymoon. Believe it or not, we actually missed our kids, yet we had an amazing time that week. Most of all, we were incredibly happy to start our life as a family.

Chapter Nine

BEAUTIFUL RESTORATION

Tania Owen

With God front and center in our marriage, life was beautiful. Though the kids were young—Chadd age nine, Tyler age seven, and Shannon age five—they got along great. Steve and I each shared joint custody of our children, so the Owen household at times felt like it had a revolving door.

Statistics show some 70 percent of blended families fail, due to difficulties in bringing up children in multiple households and with different parenting styles. Steve and I were aware of this fact, and we faced it head-on. We made a point to treat all three children as if they were *our* children. I remember telling Chadd, Tyler, and Shannon, "You know what? There are no *step* anythings in this home. No stepfather, stepmother, stepchildren, stepbrothers, or stepsister. The only steps we will recognize are those that lead from the first floor of the house to the second."

Then I spoke directly to Chadd and Tyler: "You are my children, and I will love you as if I were the mother who brought you into this earth." Of course, they had a mother who loved them, and I was always mindful to respect that relationship. I just wanted them to know how much I loved them too.

Before marrying, Steve and I had made the decision we would never talk about the other parent in front of the children, that we would purpose to always get along. We made this decision for the sake of their mental well-being. When Chadd or Tyler had a school event, we usually sat with their mother and made it a point to demonstrate for the boys a good example of family. Though things didn't work as smoothly with Shannon's father, we kept our home life positive and stable in her behalf.

It took a little time for Steve and me to work out a comfortable rhythm with regard to our different workdays and shifts, but we eventually made the schedule work. We took turns picking up the kids at school and taking them to their respective activities and sports. For the first eight years of our marriage, we maintained a steady focus on our children's lives and were as involved as other parents who had regular work schedules.

We loved participating in our children's activities, including attending Christmas plays and school awards programs, being there for Show-and-Tell, and supervising school outings. When the boys were old enough to play football, Steve helped coach their team, and I served as the team mother.

As a family we enjoyed camping together and going to Lake Powell in Arizona, where Steve had so many happy memories from his own childhood. There he taught us to water ski, and we created many wonderful memories of our own.

Of course, all of this cost money. Though both Steve and I earned good incomes, he made a conscious decision to work as much overtime as possible. He wanted to take advantage of the present abundance of available overtime because we knew at some point it would dry up. But it didn't dry up. Anytime my husband had a chance to work overtime, he took it. When he wasn't working overtime, he was coaching football or working one of his collateral assignments with the Los Angeles County Sheriff's Mounted Enforcement Detail or the Off-Road Motorcycle Team.

God had blessed us with an abundant life for which we were grateful, but over the course of several years, we had taken our eyes off Him and become so involved with life that we'd relegated Him to the backseat in our relationship and family. Of course, we still prayed over dinner and went to church together when we could, but in essence both Steve and I were living in the world.

The first time I realized Steve and I had a breach in our relationship was when I spoke to him about an issue concerning Shannon. She'd had some difficulties with her father; when she was with him in his home things didn't always run smoothly. Though Steve loved her dearly, he didn't have the emotional tools to help her with her struggle.

For instance, he found talking with Chadd and Tyler easy and natural. They had a great time as they carried on boisterous conversations about football and guy stuff. Steve had a big thunderous voice that boomed throughout the house any time he spoke, yet he had no idea how intimidating that voice could be to a young girl. There were times when Steve disciplined Shannon and his tone disturbed me, but I didn't say anything. I knew he was unaware of the impact his voice had on her, and I wanted to respect my husband.

But one day after Steve had corrected Shannon in what I felt was a particularly rough tone, I knew I had to say something. I told him I didn't want him to speak to her in that way, and I was stunned when he looked at me and said, "Fine. I'm done. You deal with it." Steve and I had never raised our voices to each other, and we didn't do so then. But in avoiding further discussion about the matter, we'd allowed a crack in the foundation of our marriage. Steve stood on one side. I stood on the other.

As Steve continued to work overtime, he often maxed out. I remember doing a lot of things by myself such as going to get-togethers with friends and spending my days off alone. But that wasn't the worst part. He worked a lot of graveyard shifts that left me sleeping alone in our bed on a frequent basis. I missed my husband and the intimacy of our relationship.

It seemed Steve prioritized everything and everyone else above me, to the extent I felt as if I weren't even married. In reality my husband wasn't doing anything wrong. He wanted to provide for us and our future, and he wanted to be a present father to our three kids. Unfortunately, I was the one person who was left behind. I wanted attention from my husband, and I wanted time when I had him to myself, but it never seemed to work out that way. Life and overtime had overtaken our lives, and I was jealous of the "other woman" in his life. Her name was *work*.

I asked Steve to stop working so much overtime because I wanted to spend more time together—with him. But he never relented. So even though we were always there—both off duty and in uniform—for all three kids, Steve's and my relationship continued to suffer.

And the crack in the foundation of our marriage continued to widen.

I resented my husband so much that I shut down emotionally, mentally, and physically, and only gave our relationship the bare minimum effort. Steve and I were disconnected, and I didn't know what to do about it. Clearly our marriage was in trouble. I desperately wanted my husband back and attempted on more than one occasion to talk to him about our relationship. Each time, the conversation became an argument, and every single time Steve put up his hand as if to say *whatever*, and then he walked away.

I was accustomed to resolving issues by discussing them, but my husband either couldn't—or wouldn't—engage verbally so that we could come to resolution. I was continually frustrated because any and all issues in our marriage remained unresolved. The matter became so ridiculous that I secretly thought of my husband as *the running man* because he always ran from conflict. How he could so boldly run toward conflict while on the job and so quickly and efficiently bring about resolution, yet in his personal life avoid conflict altogether was a mystery to me. I didn't understand it, and I had no one to talk with about the matter.

I was home alone one weekend. The kids were with their other parents, and Steve was working overtime, but then he came to the house to get something. I decided to take the unexpected opportunity to have a conversation with him. I said, "Steve, I need to talk to you about a matter."

Something in my tone got his attention. He stopped, looked at me, and said, "What's going on?"

"I'm no longer happy."

He actually appeared to be scared. "What does that mean?"

"I'm no longer happy in our marriage. I feel as though my life consists of my working all week, coming home and working all weekend, and then going back to work again. We never do anything together anymore because you choose to work overtime on my days off. Steve, I still love you, but I think we need to get some counseling as we agreed to do before we married. The way I see it, our problem is that we don't communicate."

For a moment I felt a sense of hope that we might have a breakthrough, but it was quickly dispelled when a call came over his patrol radio and he had to leave immediately. We never talked about the matter again. Steve and I continued to get along okay as we worked and remained engaged with our kids' lives. I remember thinking, *Maybe we're just going through a phase that will eventually work itself out.*

But it didn't. I was physically tired and emotionally depleted. I went through the motions of going to work, taking care of our home, and living like a single person while my husband pursued his relationship with his work. Why couldn't he love and pursue *me* as passionately as he did his job? I just wanted to feel alive again.

That's when I made a terrible mistake. As a deputy sheriff I regularly engaged with many members of our community and had developed a number of professional friendships. One of these friendships was with a single man who always made me laugh and feel good anytime we encountered each other. The more we talked, the better I felt about myself. I realized that, for the first time in years, I felt alive. Before I knew it, I was involved in an affair.

The euphoria I experienced from being with this man was like water to my parched emotions, yet at the same time I was terrified of my husband finding out what I was doing. I didn't want to leave Steve or lose him; however, being with that man was intoxicating like a drug—and I was willing to risk my marriage to get more of that drug. I justified my actions by telling myself I wasn't getting the love and attention I needed from my husband.

Steve and I had made an absolute mess of our marriage. He was busy with his girlfriend, *work*, and I was busy with the affair. Steve may have suspected something was going on, but it was no surprise he never confronted me.

Several months into the affair, Steve and I were home together one evening when my cell phone dinged, notifying me I had a text. I picked up my phone and saw a photo the man had sent of himself and his adult son on vacation together in Chicago. Along with the photo was a message that said, "Wish you were here."

Steve was seated next to me on the sofa, and before I could turn off my phone, he looked over my shoulder, took the phone from my hand, and read the message. Then he put the phone down and walked out of the room without saying a thing. I couldn't believe the next words out of my mouth: "It's not what you think!" Steve left the house for a while; when he returned, he didn't say a word about what he'd seen. He actually *never* mentioned it again. We never talked about it, just went on with our lives. As usual.

I knew without doubt I had deeply hurt my husband, yet I continued the affair. The guilt I felt for what I was doing to him made me sick to my stomach, but I was like the proverbial dog returning to her vomit. I was caught in a downward spiral and didn't know what to do. I came to hate myself, and I didn't want to live like that anymore. I wanted my marriage to return to what it had once been, and I wanted my husband, whom I loved with all my heart. I felt I would die if he ever left me. And still the affair continued.

Perhaps the most irrational emotion I experienced during that time was anger at God. I remember leaving the man's house after we'd been together and literally weeping as I drove home. I would yell at God and tell Him, "I can't do this anymore!" In one breath I'd tell Him I didn't know how to fix the situation and would beg Him to help me. In the next breath I'd demand my life back. I was so thankful my vehicle had tinted windows so that no one could see my bizarre behavior.

Steve's resentment toward me started the night he saw the text message. Instead of confronting the matter, he just dug in deeper and worked even more. Though we made love occasionally, for the most part his demeanor was standoffish. We spoke to each other politely when we were together. The smile he'd once had only for me was gone; he wasn't the husband I'd married because I'd betrayed him. The children, now all teenagers, became his focus.

The guilt and shame I felt for what I was doing to my husband and to my family had become unbearable. I felt completely alone, and I continually beat myself up. I felt no deep emotions for the man I was involved with; he was simply filling a void in my life. At some point I began to fear he would have strong feelings for me. And that's just what happened.

One day when we were together, he told me he wanted me to leave Steve. When I said I would never leave Steve because I loved him, he said, "Then what are you doing here?"

Wow—what a slap in the face those words were! I remained quiet for a minute as I looked at him and carefully thought about what he'd just said. I was stunned and felt absolutely stupid, yet I felt as if blinders had just been removed from my eyes. I'd been angry with God for not helping me, for not fixing the situation, when all along the choice to stay or go had been mine. I knew God said in His Word, *"I have set before you life and death, blessing and cursing; therefore choose life, that both you and your descendants may live"* (Deuteronomy 30:19). Before me was the choice of life or death for my marriage, and just in case I didn't know which to choose, God said to *choose life.*

I picked up my belongings and left. It was over.

Though mentally and emotionally ready to fix my marriage relationship, I understood it would be an uphill climb. Steve's resentment toward me was palpable and the breach between us wider than ever. Still, we continued to live life and get along as parents. Our relationship a standstill, at least we weren't damaging it anymore.

We had long ago established that divorce would never be an option for us, so in my mind we just needed to hang on and wait for the rollercoaster ride to come to an end. I remember thinking,

We'll get past this phase. We'd also promised each other that when the time came our marriage was in trouble, we would go to counseling. But that didn't happen.

After two years without progress, I came up with a different strategy for healing my marriage: I would simply be a better wife, a nicer wife, a more understanding wife. I tried my best, but that approach didn't seem to work. Steve frequently talked down to me, which made me feel he was yelling at me. Though he actually wasn't yelling, his voice was so big, it boomed throughout the house. One day I snapped and said, "Don't talk to me like I'm one of your subordinates. I'm your wife, and I don't deserve to be talked to that way."

Over the next two years, both Chadd and Tyler graduated from high school and entered college. I still carried tremendous guilt for what I'd done to my husband and my marriage, so I decided I'd do everything I could to spend more time with Steve. I was able to change shifts at work so that we had the same hours—surely a step in the right direction. Sadly, when we were home together Steve no longer talked to me about the cases he was working, our kids, or any of the countless other things we used to talk about on a daily basis. It had now been four years since the end of the affair, and it felt as if we were living separate lives.

Early one morning I was awakened by the sound of running water in our bathroom. Steve was already dressed and brushing his teeth. When I asked him where he was going, he replied, "To work."

"Steve, you don't start work for several hours. I changed my hours so we could spend time together." When he didn't reply, I asked, "Why don't you talk to me anymore?"

"There's nothing to talk about." He left the bedroom and went straight to the garage and spent some time lifting weights before getting into his car and leaving.

I didn't know what more to do. For the past four years I'd given my all to my husband and marriage, yet Steve had emotionally checked out of the relationship. He continued to work overtime, which meant I slept alone most of the time. Looking back, the red flags were there. I just didn't see them.

I received an email notification from my phone carrier regarding a data overage on my account that would result in an extra charge for each GB of data. I automatically assumed Shannon had again gone over the data limit, but when I spoke to her about it, she said she hadn't used much data. I figured it was a one-time matter and let it go.

When I received two subsequent notifications of overage, I decided to log in to my account to see what was going on. I first checked Shannon's number and confirmed she was telling the truth about her usage. Then I went to Steve's number. What I saw left me feeling cold as ice: page after page of calls and texts to one single number, all hours of the day and night. The sinking feeling in my stomach told me this could mean only one thing—my husband was having an affair. In a matter of seconds my world had turned upside down.

I knew I needed to get hold of my emotions. I also knew I needed to come up with a plan to find out who the person was and decide how to confront my husband. If I didn't have evidence when I confronted him, he could simply deny it. I didn't want to be accused of being crazy for suspecting something without proof.

Since I was a detective and my husband the suspect, I went to work. My first step was to call the number. When a female answered, I hung up. That was all I needed to hear. Next I used my investigative skills to find out who the woman was. Then, without Steve's knowledge, I set up the GPS on his phone so that I could track him. It took less than two weeks to gather all the information I needed. But I still needed to plan how to confront my husband.

Perhaps the wisest thing I did at the time was talk to my supervising officer, Sergeant Derek Yoshino, a Christian man whom I later referred to as my earthly angel. He and his wife prayed for us, and he also gave me godly counsel. I told Sergeant Yoshino my concern that Steve might have strong feelings for the woman. I also told him I knew I mustn't confront my husband in anger, that to do so would only cause him to walk away.

My sergeant advised that after I confronted Steve, I needed to make sure he left the house. I knew my sergeant was right, but the thought of actually bringing Steve's affair to light had made me an emotional mess, so I was thankful Sergeant Yoshino gave me four days off to deal with the matter.

I picked the day to confront my husband and made sure Shannon would not be at home. I didn't want her exposed to our problems. The boys were away at college, so Steve and I had the house to ourselves that morning when I told him I wanted to talk to him. I could tell I'd caught him off guard, and he seemed a bit nervous and suspicious. When I asked him to take a seat, he did, though I was much too nervous to sit down myself. Above all, I wanted to remain calm.

"Steve, I know you are having an affair, and you need to stop it right now." He didn't say anything, so I continued. "I know who she is, where she lives, and where she works." Maintaining my composure, I told him everything I'd found out and presented him with the supporting paperwork.

He was quiet for a moment, and then he asked, "How did you know?" I told him about the notice I'd received from my carrier concerning data overages. At that point Steve had no choice but to acknowledge the affair. When he did, I felt as if I'd been gut-punched; my worst nightmare had just been confirmed. It was possible I was about to lose my husband to another woman, yet I had to keep myself together.

The next hurdle was the hardest for me. "Steve, you need to leave this house."

"You can't tell me to leave. This is my house!"

I remained perfectly calm. "You need to go to a neutral location to think because you have a decision to make. Either you stay with me or you move forward with her. It's your choice. Don't come back here because you pity me; come back only if you want to make this marriage work. If you choose her, we'll split everything fifty-fifty and go on with our lives."

Steve didn't leave right away. We actually talked, and I learned why he had started the affair. I didn't want him to leave, but it needed to happen. If he was going to stay with me, I wanted his decision to be purposeful, not made out of a sense of obligation.

I couldn't believe it: for the first time in our marriage we had just *completed* a conversation about our problems and had come to a conclusion. Though I was calm on the outside, I was dying on the inside. By asking my husband to leave, I had essentially handed him over on a silver platter to the other woman. As I watched him pack his bag, my emotions finally got the best of me. I could no longer contain my pain.

I started bawling and told Steve that I loved him, that I didn't want him to leave. "We can work on this," I cried. He too became emotional, but then he told me it was too late. I realized I needed to give him space, so I stood aside as he picked up his bag and left the house. I'd never felt more alone in my life. I knew whatever happened next was out of my control.

I had a sleepless night as thoughts of Steve being with the other woman ran through my mind. I felt so physically ill the following morning that I could barely down a cup of coffee. The day passed in a fog of fear, sorrow, and thoughts of *what if?* What if Steve chose the other woman? What if I have to go through life alone? What if I have to see him regularly at work?

I was lying on the sofa in a darkened room late that evening when I heard the garage door open. Excitement filled my being as I wondered, *Is my husband coming back to me? Are we going to get a second chance at our marriage?* I jumped up and raced to the garage where Steve was standing, his bag in hand. The moment we locked eyes, I swear we had a full conversation without uttering a word. I knew this wasn't the time to start a conversation; we'd just had one. He looked as miserable and spent as I did, so I simply said, "Let's go to bed."

The minute we placed our heads on the pillows, we fell asleep, Steve on his side of the bed and me on mine. Our emotions were shot.

Over coffee the next morning, Steve told me he was back and wanted to make things work. I said we needed to start by meeting with the other woman so that in my presence he could tell her things were over between them. He said that *because* the affair was over, he didn't want to meet with her again. I didn't force the issue; rather, I chose to believe him.

Though in the coming days we still weren't communicating, I decided I would win my husband over by doing everything I could to be the best wife possible. Instead of throwing what had happened in his face and accusing him, I would maintain the peace in our marriage and in our house. Yet what I felt was anything but peace. My stomach still felt as if it were tied in a knot. I couldn't eat and quickly lost fifteen pounds, barely existing on two hundred calories a day.

From my perspective, Steve's unwillingness to talk about our issues meant he wasn't putting forth an effort to work on our marriage. I felt he was neither committed to me nor was he back with me 100%. I couldn't concentrate while I was at work because my mind was focused on personal issues. I was worrying myself sick, wondering if Steve was going to see the other woman again. I didn't realize it, but there was an all-out assault going on against my mind. The enemy had me so bound up with thoughts of Steve and the woman that I came to the point of hatred.

I've heard it said that there's a fine line between love and hate, but I didn't realize how true that was until I lived it. Though I loved Steve with all my heart, because of where we were in our relationship—and the fact that the enemy was having a field day in my mind—I also hated him. I wanted to destroy my husband, obliterate him because of what he'd done.

Prior to our marriage we'd said we would never divorce. Now we'd both been involved in affairs. But in my mind, there was a difference between my affair and Steve's. I'd never given my heart to the man I'd been involved with; I'd kept a wall up while I filled an emotional void in my life. Through my clouded perspective I believed Steve had betrayed me by becoming emotionally involved with another woman, and that's why I was mad.

The more I thought about Steve and the other woman, the more pain I felt in my stomach. When I began to hyperventilate, I realized I was having panic attacks. Here I was, a first responder who couldn't even help herself. Now in this mental state, how was I supposed to help others?

That's when I decided I would confront the woman—oh how I wanted to hurt her for what *she* had done! When I confided in my sergeant what I planned to do, he said, "Tania, it's not worth it. *She's* not worth it. What would it do to your career if you attacked a civilian?"

I knew he was right, but I was still angry when I got home that night. Steve was working and I was alone with my thoughts, which grew darker and darker by the minute. *I'll kill Steve, and then I'll kill her. But should I kill myself too or instead go to prison for the rest of my life?* I was in a deep pit, held captive by the horrifying thoughts that bombarded my mind, and I didn't know how to get out. But then I saw my Bible.

I opened it and read these words: *For though we walk in the flesh, we do not war according to the flesh. For the weapons of our warfare are not carnal but mighty in God for the pulling down of strongholds, casting down arguments and every high thing that exalts itself against the knowledge of God, bringing every thought into captivity to the obedience of Christ* (Ephesians 10:3–5).

That's when I fell to my knees and cried out to God. "What am I doing? I'm out of control. I need you, Jesus—help me!" In an instant I felt as if a weight was lifted from my shoulders and blinders removed from my eyes. I realized how thoughts of vengeance, of taking the lives of others, had been controlling me. Had I actually yielded to the thoughts of murder that had bombarded my mind I would have essentially left our three children without parents. And what of the other woman? What of her family and loved ones?

I continued reading my Bible, turning the pages back to the fifth chapter of Ephesians.

> For you were once darkness, but now you are light in the Lord. Walk as children of light (for the fruit of the Spirit is in all goodness, righteousness, and truth), finding out what is acceptable to the Lord. And have no fellowship with the unfruitful works of darkness, but rather expose them. For it is shameful even to speak of those things which are done by them in secret. But all things that are exposed are made manifest by the light, for whatever makes manifest is light. Therefore He says: "Awake, you who sleep, arise from the dead, and Christ will give you light" (Ephesians 5:8–14).

In an instant God delivered me out of the darkness that had held me in such torment and despair and into the light of His love.

If He did this for me, then He would surely also do it for my husband. I needed to take my hands off the matter and trust Him, but that was easier said than done.

A few weeks later, I was working the late shift one Monday, and Steve was on his day off. When I called to ask how he was doing, Steve told me he was going into the office. I asked why he wanted to do that on his day off, and he said he was behind on his paperwork. I didn't have a good feeling about the situation. I waited an hour to give him time to get to his desk, and then I called him. He didn't answer, so I left a message. He didn't return my call.

Immediately a familiar wave of fear and suspicion hit me. I still had the GPS tracker on his phone, so I checked it. He was at a restaurant just a block from *her* house. I felt something snap, followed by a burning rage inside me as dark thoughts again bombarded my mind. I knew exactly where they were, and I thought how easy it would be just to drive over there, pull up in my vehicle, and go inside and murder them. I felt as if I was about to go off the deep end, but I reminded myself I was at work and had a job to do. I also reminded myself that my greater desire was to see my husband delivered from darkness just as I had been.

The next few hours seemed an eternity. I told my sergeant what was going on and shared my feelings. He prayed for me and gave me some words of wisdom. By the time my shift ended, I'd calmed down considerably.

On the drive home I prayed, asking God to give me the words to say to my husband. When I arrived at the house at 2:30 a.m., I still didn't know what I was going to say. I felt as if I'd been played for a fool, and I decided I was no longer going to be a doormat in an effort to get my husband to love me. It was time to put my foot down—I was done walking on eggshells. Steve and I were going to have a real conversation about what our life was going to look like moving forward.

I didn't bother to change out of uniform when I walked into our bedroom. This matter needed to be addressed immediately. I could tell Steve was pretending to be asleep, so I pulled up a chair as close as I could to his side of the bed, sat down, and stared at him until he opened his eyes.

"You've disappointed me. I thought we were going to work on our marriage."

A puzzled expression came across his face. He sat up and in a disgusted tone said, "What are you talking about?"

Though it wasn't true, I said, "I got a phone call today from someone who saw you with her." Steve immediately went into defense mode, denying they'd been together. In hopes the GPS location had been accurate, I told him to stop the denials, and then I gave the name of the restaurant. As I held my breath and waited for his response, I could almost see the wheels turning in his head.

Suddenly Steve's entire demeanor changed. His body appeared to deflate as he uncrossed his arms and said, "Yes, I was with her."

I was done playing the role of a mouse to win Steve over. I felt strong and in possession of my dignity when I said, "What are we going to do?"

He didn't have an answer, so I gave him mine. "You are going to choose how you want to spend the rest of your life. Let's take a look at reality: You aren't caught in a marriage where, if you leave, you'll have to pay spousal or child support. There's nothing that binds us together financially, and as I told you before, we can split everything fifty-fifty and go our separate ways. So again, I ask you, what are we going to do?"

In truth, we weren't in the mess we were in solely because of Steve; we'd *both* botched up what was once a beautiful marriage, life, and family.

But then something happened. My husband—the strong, beautiful, bad-ass cop I had known—completely broke down. I wanted so badly to take him in my arms and tell him I loved him, but I didn't. I knew if we were to save our marriage, I had to stand strong and immoveable on one critical issue: we were going to counseling.

We were referred to a wonderful Christian counselor at a nearby church, Pastor Mark, who had experience in dealing with marriage issues. The first thing he did when we initially met with him was pray over us and our marriage. I knew immediately we were back home where we belonged—with God.

Throughout the counseling process my heart never hardened toward my husband, and I still loved him. Even so, the enemy had me bound in emotional chains that made me feel as if one moment I loved Steve with every fiber of my being and the next moment I loathed him. I can't even begin to describe the intense spiritual warfare taking place inside me.

Pastor Mark helped me realize the woman Steve had been with was not at fault. She was merely the endgame to the mess Steve and I had created. I took full responsibility for my actions, for not being the wife Steve had needed me to be when we'd started having problems. The Bible says, *For we do not wrestle against flesh and blood, but against principalities, against powers, against the rulers of darkness of this age, against spiritual hosts of wickedness in the heavenly places* (Ephesians 6:12). Instead of aggressively confronting the enemy, whom Jesus said comes *"to steal, and to kill, and to destroy"* (John 10:10), I had foolishly given in to the devil and had seen my husband as my enemy. I'm sure Steve experienced similar feelings toward me as he too struggled with his faith.

Pastor Mark led us to James 4:7 that says, *Therefore submit to God. Resist the devil and he will flee from you* and to 2 Corinthians 10:5 that says, *Casting down arguments and every high thing that exalts itself against the knowledge of God, bringing every thought into captivity to the obedience of Christ.* Pastor Mark also taught us that *the weapons of our warfare are not carnal but mighty in God for pulling down strongholds* (v. 4).

Armed with the Word of God and renewed faith in Jesus Christ, we slowly began to right our sinking marriage. One of the best decisions I made was to respect my husband at all times throughout that difficult season. No matter what emotions I was dealing with, I never spoke ill of him to anyone, nor did I ever insult him. As I knew all too well, once I hurt the person I loved with words, I could never take those words back. The choice was mine, either to speak words of love and affirmation, or words of hate and vengeance. Once I chose words of love, I began to experience an emotion I'd not felt for a very long time—hope.

When Steve and I opened up to each other and truly began to talk, things changed rapidly. We knew the key to healing and wholeness was *forgiveness*. We'd already gone through the process of asking God to forgive us of our sins; the next thing we did was forgive each other for the pain we'd caused. Finally, through many tears, each of us forgave ourselves, which was perhaps the hardest thing of all. We surrendered to each other, and together we surrendered to almighty God.

The moment we submitted to God, I let go of everything: all the pain, the guilt, and the burden I'd carried for years. And God took it all from me. I was free! Jesus truly had carried all that pain when He died for all mankind on that cross over two thousand years ago. What an amazing and loving God we have. My once-broken heart was now whole, completely open to love my husband again.

I told Steve I wanted to be an honoring wife to him, the wife he needed me to be. I apologized for failing him as a wife, and he apologized for failing me as a husband.

Steve and I made the decision to forget—and I mean *forget*—all the pain we'd caused each other. We agreed never to bring it up again; rather, with the help of God, we agreed we'd be kind to ourselves and start from scratch. After all, He loved us so much, He gave us a second chance. Two of my favorite Bible verses at that time were, *I can do all things through Christ who strengthens me* (Philippians 4:13) and *"So I will restore to you the years that the swarming locust has eaten"* (Joel 2:25).

God was indeed true to His promise to restore our marriage. For the next four years before Steve went home to be with the Lord, I experienced the most amazing love for and from my husband. He'd fallen back in love with me, and I with him. I can honestly say I loved him more than on the day I married him.

During those years, we learned to communicate effectively, share our feelings, and listen to each other. I didn't mind being in second place in Steve's life, for he'd put God first. Steve never worked overtime on my days off; instead, we oftentimes hopped on the motorcycle and drove wherever the road led us. We enjoyed spending quality time together and focusing on each other. In addition, we returned to praying together, daily asking the Lord to bless our marriage, home, and family.

Each Sunday morning before church, Steve served me breakfast in bed, and while I ate, he read from the Bible. We also had our own mini-Bible study. An added blessing, as Steve and I grew closer and stronger in the Lord, we watched our children's relationships with the Lord grow and mature, and we became stronger and closer as a family. We were all back in the Word of God.

Steve and I often discussed our jobs and the extreme dangers we routinely faced. I recalled how, when Steve and I had worked together, he'd been like a bulldog, never backing down from any situation. I asked him one day, "When kicking a door open or when going over a wall in pursuit of a suspect, do you ever, for one second, hesitate and think the person might be on the other side, lying in wait for you with a gun?"

"Absolutely not," he said with such force that I asked him why not. "Because I feel God is with me." He paused and then added, "Hon, if it's my time to go home, it's my time to go, so I don't worry about it."

I chose not to worry about it either. If Steve had peace, then so did I.

The Sunday before Steve was murdered, the sermon was titled "Why Do Bad Things Happen to Good People?" After the service, one of the band members whose brother was in law enforcement asked me if I ever feared for my husband's safety on the job. I quickly responded to her, "No, I don't. He's in God's hands."

Three days later Steve was murdered.

When I next went to church, despite all that was going on in our lives, I made a point to find her. "I recall our last conversation," I told her, "and I want you to know, I still don't worry about my husband—he's *still* in God's hands."

I know my husband prayed over me a lot. He was a loving and beautiful man. A wife knows the integrity of her husband, who he is at his core. Steve was caring, kind, humble, loving, a protector, a grizzly bear (and a Teddy bear), an incredible father, a provider, and an amazing and romantic husband. That is why I chose to fight for our marriage.

And best of all, he chose me—*me*—to be his wife. I feel so proud and honored to call myself Mrs. Steve Owen.

Part Three

AFTERMATH

But we have this treasure in earthen vessels, that the excellence of the power may be of God and not of us. We are hard-pressed on every side, yet not crushed; we are perplexed, but not in despair; persecuted, but not forsaken; struck down, but not destroyed.

2 CORINTHIANS 4:7–9

Chapter Ten

FIRST STEPS FORWARD

Tania and Vickie

VICKIE

I don't believe anyone is ever prepared to lose a spouse, no matter how that loss occurs. As humans we are all unique individuals with our own personalities and thought processes. There is no one-size-fits-all manual, no set of universal guidelines on how to handle these issues. We all deal with them differently.

I never thought in a million years that at a young age I would be without my husband. Like most couples, we had a plan for our life together. Our five-year plan included retirement, moving, and other accomplishments we'd dreamed of. We both assumed those plans would happen, but then came the life-changing event of my losing Mitch. I struggled to wrap my mind around the fact he was gone—he'd gone home—and I was left in a world turned upside down. The beautiful future we'd planned was no longer a reality.

What was blatantly real at the time was the constant sense of being in a proverbial fog. I don't remember a lot about the initial weeks and months following Mitch's passing. I can't recall much about his memorial service. I couldn't tell you where I was for those first holidays without him or what I did New Year's Eve.

My biggest struggle was that I couldn't remember the most routine things about everyday life: Did I eat? What time did I wake up? Did I make this month's mortgage payment? I'd always been an organized, on-top-of-things person, but that was no longer the norm. It was probably a year before I felt semi-human again.

When I say there's no book on dealing with loss, I'm also talking about practical matters such as when it was time to clean out my house or when I should give my husband's things away. I knew I had to move forward in my life, but those first steps weren't easy. They didn't feel normal. I remember asking myself these questions: What is my new normal? What is normal now? I didn't have answers, but one thing I did know was that I needed to heal (though I wasn't even sure what that meant).

I found that people were all too eager to offer advice on these matters. Though their comments were well intended, I can honestly say it would have been better had those thoughts been kept unspoken. I can't count the times I heard people say something such as, "Well, if it were me, this is what I would do …" In truth, none of us have any idea what we would do if we were in another's situation, so it's best we keep unsolicited advice to ourselves.

One of the reasons Mitch married me was that I am a strong woman, and in my husband's wisdom he did what he could to prepare me to continue living successfully without him. But we live in a tough world. I learned that my no longer being part of a unit with a spouse changed everything. Yet those who have never experienced such a loss feel they have all the answers and are too eager to tell you

- what you should do and how you should act.
- what you should and shouldn't buy.
- where you should live and when you should or shouldn't move.
- what you should or shouldn't wear and how you should style your hair.
- when and whom you should date.

I found there was a lot of outside noise and chatter that was absolutely no help. I was a heartbroken, shattered woman who'd just lost the love of my life, and I was trying to figure out how to do life alone and be okay with it. To this day I still ask myself, *Am I doing the right thing? Am I living the way Mitch wanted me to live? Am I honoring him?* These are the measures I use as I continue to build my new life, but most importantly I ask myself, *Am I happy?* I know my happiness is what Mitch wanted most for me.

TANIA

For those who have never lost a spouse, I'd like to paint a picture of what grief looked like to me. I have no idea what it's like to lose a child, so not for one second will I attempt to address that kind of grief. But Vickie and I have both lost our husbands, and we hope our words will bring comfort to others who have experienced such a loss.

When I lost Steve, and Vickie subsequently lost Mitch, all four of us were near the age of retirement. God had healed both marriages to the point they were essentially in a state of perfection. That perfection was a result of God's grace. We had raised our children, and they were either already living on their own or were about to. Both couples looked forward to retirement and enjoying the next season of our lives.

As for my marriage to Steve, I like to say all the planets were aligned, our finances were great, and everything was perfect. We were ready to retire and live out our dreams. We'd worked hard throughout our careers in law enforcement, and Steve had made great financial planning decisions for us. We'd kiddingly told our children that when we retired, we would move to another state. Of course, we'd come back to visit our grandkids.

But then on October 5, 2016, everything changed. It wasn't my husband and I walking toward our future together; it was just me. When I returned home after the harrowing events of that day, it was to an empty bedroom. Steve had been my rock, my world, my everything. When I'd fallen, he'd picked me up. When I'd needed love, he'd given it to me. When I'd wanted advice, he'd offered it freely. When I'd needed anything, he'd been there for me. Now, the most important person in my life—the man I had lived for—was gone. I learned the truth of the saying that when you lose a spouse, half of you is gone.

The biggest challenge for me in taking those first steps forward was the abject loneliness. My husband was no longer there to lie down next to me, to hold me, to kiss me and say, "Babe, I love you. We'll get through this together." Of course, I was blessed to have wonderful friends and family, but they couldn't provide the intimacy only my husband could give.

I remember once explaining this to a male friend, who responded, saying, "Well, Tania, I'll give you a hug." That was not the kind of intimacy I wanted—he had no idea of the level of intimacy I so desperately missed. Such as sitting down together after dinner, enjoying a glass of wine and a movie. Now it was just me, and I had no one to talk to.

VICKIE

After being part of a married couple for so many years, the transition to being a single girl again isn't easy. Mitch and I had had a group of married couples we were accustomed to being with, but meeting with them was no longer enjoyable because I now felt like a third wheel. Socializing with couples only served to remind me of what my life *used* to be like. I loved them and knew they were my friends, but the common denominator of being part of a couple no longer existed for me.

One decision I made almost immediately after Mitch passed was to go off social media. There are both good people and not-so-good people in this world; the latter were quick to post judgmental opinions about me. Worse yet were the men who didn't have a problem only three days after Mitch passed to feel out the situation, so to speak.

I'd been warned about these unwanted contacts from men I didn't know who would figure out I'd recently lost my husband. I hate the word *widow*, and I refuse to use it. I'm not a widow—I am still Mitch Speed's wife.

I've learned to be protective of both my private life and my son. I'm guarded about my friendships, which I am deliberate to establish in a spirit of trust. And that trust runs very deep—as it does with my relationship with Tania, who has become family to me.

One of the Bible stories that means so much to Tania and me is that of Ruth and Naomi. Both women had lost their husbands and subsequently made the choice to move forward in life together. In Ruth 1:16 we see these familiar words Ruth spoke to Naomi:

> "Entreat me not to leave you,
> Or to turn back from following after you;
> For wherever you go, I will go;
> And wherever you lodge, I will lodge;
> Your people shall be my people,
> And your God, my God."

Tania and I draw great comfort from this verse, knowing we are still the women our husbands knew, loved, and married. I believe Mitch and Steve are extremely happy with the decisions we are making as a family, as sisters in the Lord.

TANIA

Remember, we have peace about our decisions because we had each had discussions with our husbands about the time when one of us would have to continue in life alone. Both Steve and Mitch gave their blessing to move forward, to live our lives to the fullest, and—if we so chose—to marry again.

We have since learned the value in telling a spouse it's okay to move forward following the other one's death (though it isn't a comfortable conversation). We've encountered many women who, after grieving for their deceased husbands for ten years, still can't move forward because they feel doing so would dishonor their marriages.

Steve and Mitch wanted Vickie and me to live our lives—and live them well. Both men are now irrevocably home with the Lord, where they want to be. We honor our husbands as we move forward in the Lord, glorifying Him in serving others.

VICKIE

I know Mitch isn't here, and he isn't coming back. For me the resulting loss and grief has been the worst pain I've felt in my life. As humans we understand what it's like to feel pain when a loved one hurts us or something sad happens. But the loss of a spouse is final, a shattering of life in which the pieces will not come back together again.

My analogy is that when Mitch died, my heart was shattered into a million pieces. Over time I felt the pieces start to come together but the cracks are still there, and I can feel them. Eventually those cracks scab; however, it doesn't take much for that scab to be ripped off. This ripping can be caused by anything: Mitch's birthday, holidays without him, a song, or even the smallest things that no one can understand—sometimes not even me.

In the early days following my loss, I had so many questions: Will this wound ever heal? Will the pain that comes with breathing ever stop? When will the weight of grief become lighter? Am I going to feel this way the rest of my life? Perhaps this is why the Lord spoke these words about the Messiah through the prophet Isaiah: *Surely He has born our griefs and carried our sorrows ... The chastisement of our peace was upon Him, and by His stripes we are healed* (Isaiah 53:4–5).

Having clung to the truth of this verse, I can now say that my heart is no longer shattered, though it is still broken and cracked. But I do believe that crack will eventually become a scar, and with that scar I will continue to move forward. The pain isn't as deep as it once was, and I know I can go on in peace now, for the Bible says, *And the peace of God, which surpasses all understanding, will guard your hearts and minds through Christ Jesus* (Philippians 4:7).

TANIA

Though we began this chapter with the statement that nobody is ever prepared to lose a spouse, Vickie and I encourage not only law-enforcement families but all families to realize there are practical steps they can now take to lessen the adverse impact of future loss.

I spent three decades as a law-enforcement officer, but I am first and foremost a mother. And it is from my role as a mother that I speak to other mothers and law-enforcement wives: Have an honest conversation with your husband about your wishes should one of you pass. It's as simple as beginning with these questions: If you should pass, what would you want me to tell the children? What would you want me to do? How would you want me to handle your service? Do you want to be buried or cremated?

Something Steve and I talked about but regrettably never did was to write a letter to each of our children and leave it in the safe. Should something have happened to one or both of us, this letter would have informed them of our wishes for them and how they were to handle any related practical family matters. Of particular importance to Steve and me was that our children not be mad at God.

I am so thankful Steve and I learned never to leave for work if one or both of us were angry about something. This practice was one of the blessings that came as a result of God healing our marriage. We'd always taught our children not to leave the house without saying *I love you* and giving family members a bear hug, an Owen family tradition they carried into adulthood. I am comforted in the knowledge that in the days prior to the tragic events of October 5, 2016, we'd each given Steve a bear hug and said *I love you* to him.

I now tell law-enforcement spouses to love their husbands or wives as if today is their last day. These brave men and women leave their homes to put their lives on the line each and every day. Sadly, some don't return at the end of their shifts. I gave my husband a kiss on the morning of October 5 and said, "I love you and I'll see you tonight." That was the day he didn't come home.

VICKIE

My circumstances were different from Tania's in that I had twenty-six months to prepare for Mitch's passing. Yet nothing prepared me for the dual-parenting role I had to play where our son was concerned.

Of course, I could never replace Mitch or take the place of Brodie's father, nor have I ever wanted to. However, following an incident that occurred only weeks after Mitch passed—one that Brodie later describes in his own words—I realized my need to be more in tune with my son, more aware of what was going on in his life.

For me personally, I had to dig deep concerning my healing and how I was going to move forward, which is the reason I made the decision in August 2018 to go to counseling. I saw a therapist regularly for the eleven months preceding the first anniversary of Mitch's passing. I needed to be the best mom to my son, but I felt as if I weren't whole. Without guidance on how to be whole again, I knew I could fail as a mother.

I understand some people choose not to seek counsel, but for me seeing a professional was one of the best decisions I made at that vulnerable and difficult time. The help I received made me a better mom, and for that I am grateful.

With or without counseling, it is vital that following the loss of a spouse, one looks first and foremost to God. I don't know where I would be today without Him, and for those who don't yet know Him, my advice is to find Him and stay in faith. My heavenly Father is my source of strength and is always there when I need Him. When my heart was broken and I wondered how I was going to make it without my husband, if the pain I felt would ever go away, and what my future alone looked like, I would feel God's comfort and peace as I heard Him say, *For I know the thoughts and plans that I have for you, … thoughts and plans for welfare and peace and not for evil, to give you hope in your final outcome* (Jeremiah 29:11 AMPC).

TANIA

Vickie and I weren't the only ones who had to deal with taking first steps forward following our husbands' deaths. Our children also had to learn to find their way in life following the loss of their fathers. One thing I learned as a mother was the importance of acknowledging my children's loss and saying to them, "I'm so sorry you've lost your father."

People often ask Vickie and me how our children are doing. When we told them about our plans to publish our stories, Brodie, Shannon, and Chadd asked if they could share theirs as well. We believe their candidly honest narratives will provide practical insight into the realities of losing a parent and, at the same time, give hope for the future.

Their stories are now presented with love from our family to yours.

Chapter Eleven

A FOUNDATION OF FAITH AND LOVE

Brodie Speed

Where does one even begin to write about losing his father?

First and foremost, my name is James Brodie Speed and I'm the proud son of James Mitchell Speed and Vickie Speed. I'm not a writer like my father was, I'm a math teacher so please bear with me. My father was truly an incredible man, and I pray some of his God-given ability to touch people with his words will flow through me as I share some of my own trials, emotions, and who I am in hopes of helping you in some way.

If I learned anything about writing from my father, it's what a healing tool words can be. That's why I want to share how I've been doing since losing him on July 7, 2018, to stage-4 prostate cancer. I want to be real with you about the emotions that come with such a loss.

Cancer is the infamous C-word that we don't usually think about twice until it personally affects our own families. I remember the day my dad was diagnosed as if it were yesterday. I'd been living with some family members while attending school and had decided to move home for a few weeks to land a job prior to starting graduate school. Little did I know that move was just the start of God's plan for me and my family.

My father had been feeling a little run down and not himself. In other words, he wasn't his usual Mitch Speed self, running through life at 100 mph chasing bad guys with his seemingly never-ending childlike energy. Dad was always like Superman to me. Because he'd never had a problem with motivation, Mom and I knew something was wrong.

The doctor had run some routine tests to get to the root of the problem, and in the days we waited for the results some good old-fashioned WebMD online research pointed to an inflamed prostate, which could be resolved with less stress and a change to the diet. Once the tests were back, Mom, Dad, and I went together to learn the results. As we sat waiting for the doctor to talk to us, my mind was on a million dumb things, confident that because Superman never gets hurt our lives would soon be back to normal. But within moments after the doctor entered the room, he uttered the word *cancer*. I don't remember what he said next because I was in such shock that I couldn't focus.

At some point he asked my parents if they had any questions. I had only one question, which I thought to myself: *How long until I lose my father?* I was a young man about to enter graduate school, in essence just scraping the tip of my career. The last thing on my mind was that I had any chance of losing my father. The loss of a parent is something that happens when you're older, not when you are in your twenties.

Over the coming weeks I prayed for my father every night until God removed my fear of losing him. I reasoned that if bullets hadn't taken him out while he was on the job, surely something like cancer wouldn't do it. Anyway, the doctor said his life expectancy was between five and ten years, which meant he would see me graduate, get married, and probably hold his first grandchild. Being a grandfather may have been Mitch Speed's ultimate goal and calling from God; after all, he was just a giant kid himself.

Life changed for me and my family throughout the next two and a half years, beginning with a period of my father's strength and hope that permanently changed the trajectory of our lives. My faith in God became stronger because, frankly, it was all I had. My priorities changed. I sacrificed being closer to school and starting my career so that I could stay at home. I knew there was only one thing that mattered: family. I enjoyed countless morning talks, lunches, and laughs with my father as I learned that one aspect of losing someone over a period of time means there's no holding back, we couldn't afford to leave anything unsaid. I got to say goodbye to my father in a unique and personal way, which I will forever carry with me.

As time passed I could see my father slowing down. The original 5- to 10-year life expectancy turned to 4–5 years, which meant maybe no grandkids, but I thought surely he'd see me graduate and get married.

I will always hold Father's Day 2018 as one of the most important days of my life. My dad was bedridden at the time, so I spent the day hanging by his bedside. In the middle of the day we had one final heart-to-heart conversation. I knew how much he loved me and how proud he was of me, but I will forever appreciate those moments of hearing it again. Dad and I are both quite the emotional men, so there were lots of tears, laughs, and love.

I told him how thankful I was for all he had done, and I promised I would continue to make him proud. I told him he would always be my best friend, my role model, and the greatest father a boy could ask for. I will forever hold on to that moment.

On July 7, 2018, I was in the back room watching television by myself. Dad's body was in a state of shutting down and he'd been unresponsive for some time. He was ready to go home, but Mom and I knew he could feel our love so we continued to talk to him. Just as the UFC fight I'd been watching came to an end, Mom stepped into the room and told me I should come say my last goodbyes to Dad. With Mom and I on each side of his bed, my father took his last breath. The moment he passed my emotions became absolutely calm; I knew it was now my turn to take care of our family.

A FOUNDATION OF FAITH AND LOVE

The next few weeks were a whirlwind mixture of messages from everyone, preparing for Dad's memorial service, and trying to figure out the new life ahead for my mother and me. I have an ability to stay calm and collected in times of crisis and see to it that all those around me are taken care of, so I made sure to do just that. It's a good quality to have—unless you are unaware of suppressing your own hurt and pain. Then the good quality becomes a deadly tool.

Truth be bold, the day my father died a part of me died with him. This doesn't mean I'm a broken person; rather, a part of me will always be missing. Losing a parent or someone close does something to you that cannot fully be put into words. It breaks you down, makes you question things, and ultimately challenges you in ways you never thought possible.

At the time of this writing my dad has been gone for over two years, and I've finally started to find my path and my way back to a semi-normal life after hitting a lot of highs and lows along the way. There are no books about what to do when you lose your dad because, frankly, we all take our own paths. I'm a very introverted person, so sharing my pain and hurt with others isn't something I'm good at. As an only child, I am skilled at dealing with my problems and relying on myself to get through it all.

Shortly after my dad's passing, when friends and family texted or emailed me to ask how I was doing, I'd respond with a short generic message to let them know I was handling it and I'd be okay. But in the back of my head I envisioned myself as one of those cinematic characters who snapped, going off on an epic rant: "I just lost my father—do you *really* need to ask how I'm doing?"

I learned it was hard to face reality and the resulting emotions; it was much easier to hide the scars. But then, on August 10, I went face to face with my demons. Throughout college I'd struggled with drinking. I don't mean to imply I was alcoholic; rather I hadn't learned to drink responsibly. For instance, I'd often drink in my room before going out to a party or a bar and then drive home under the influence, putting myself in danger more times than I'd like to admit.

On the night of August 10, I'd gone out for a few drinks with a friend, whom I'd agreed to drive home when we were done. We'd driven less than half a mile after leaving the bar when I saw those dreaded red-and-blue lights in my rearview mirror. As if life hadn't given me enough to deal with, the next thing I knew I was sitting in the back of a cop car—handcuffed. My decision to drink that night had nothing to do with coping with the loss of my father; rather, it was a decision I'd made too many times, which had now caught up with me.

God has a funny way of keeping us in check. The Bible says, *"And you shall know the truth, and the truth shall make you free"* (John 8:32). I had been running from my emotions after the loss of my father, and now time was up for me. I was about to learn a lesson the hard way.

The California Highway Patrol took me in, charged me with a DUI, and transported me to the Lancaster Station. I was about to spend the night in jail at the station where my father had made a name and built a reputation that was an example for others to follow. After the initial shock of my predicament wore off, I was booked and then they walked me down to the cell where I would remain until morning.

I'd been to this station hundreds of times throughout my life. I'd walked almost every inch of it with my father as he bragged about me and showed me off to his friends. But now I was in an area I'd never seen before, my very presence an announcement to the world that I'd hit rock bottom.

The door shut behind me and I sat down on the bed. It was as if the rest of the world stopped in that moment. I lost it as every bit of pain and every emotion I'd shoved down came rushing to the surface. I sat alone and cried as I went through the lowest moment of my life. Less than one month ago I'd stood at my father's service and talked about proudly carrying on the Speed name. Now here I was sitting in a jail cell at the station where that name had earned its honorable reputation.

As painful as that night was, the slap of reality was just what I needed. I realized I was *not* okay and that the way to wholeness was a long road ahead of me. I'm not proud of the decision I made to drink that night, but I'm grateful for the lesson I learned that set me on the path toward healing.

I was referred to a therapist so that those concerned for me could be assured I didn't have alcoholic tendencies or that I was facing real harm. Those three mandatory sessions showed me that I had some hurdles to get past. First and foremost would be to face the loss of my dad and discuss it with someone who could help me.

It took a year before I was ready to move forward, but finally on a Tuesday afternoon in an empty parking lot, without anyone else's knowledge, I made the move and found a therapist to help me tackle my loss. I attended therapy for months without telling a soul. I wanted to address my issues on my own, at my own pace, and at my own comfort level. And that's exactly what I did. I'm not a perfect person and I still struggle with the loss of my father. But now, when people ask how I'm doing, I can honestly say, "Not the best—but I'm getting better every day."

Losing my dad permanently changed me. As I said, a little piece of me died the day he died. I lost a little bit of my joy, a little bit of my goofy side, and a little bit of me will never be the same.

I struggled with depression following my DUI because it was the first time I was forced to face my emotions. I lost my appetite, couldn't sleep, and wouldn't work out. I lacked motivation for myself.

Though going to therapy helped, I still experience emotional highs and lows as I go through the never-ending process of adapting and rolling with the punches. I still have days when I am sad and depressed; getting out of bed is hard to do with a broken heart, and I have moments when I cry my eyes out in my car. Some days are easier, but others require a lot of "sucking it up," putting on a smile and not letting the world know I am heartbroken.

My dad was my best friend, my role model, my hero, and the man I want to be. Losing him was something I didn't expect to happen until he was old and gray. Some days I still don't understand how this was part of God's plan, and I wonder why it didn't happen to someone who was a bad person.

A FOUNDATION OF FAITH AND LOVE

I have moments when I experience every emotion under the sun: I feel cheated. I feel hurt. I feel that I don't deserve this, and I feel angry. But I've come to realize it's okay to feel these emotions. I'll never understand why God chose to take my dad from me. He didn't deserve this and, being honest, my mother and I didn't deserve to be left on our own.

I was lucky enough to see how much God used my dad, and all the good that came from his story, yet it still doesn't seem fair to me. Some days I feel cheated by God. My kids won't get to meet their grandfather, he will never get to meet my future wife, he won't be there to see me get married, and he won't be there to help me be a better man, husband, and father. He won't be there to get old and gray with my mom and drive me crazy when he retires. I struggle with the reality that I was robbed of those moments and opportunities, which can never be replaced.

My current struggle is with the big moments in life, my father's birthday being the most recent when a wave of emotion came crashing down on me. I woke up that morning and remained in my bed and cried for an hour because I didn't want to face the day. I felt as if my wound had been healing, but someone had ripped off the scab and caused it to start bleeding all over again. I now realize that these are the moments when I will struggle most as I move forward: the day I get engaged or married, the day I find out I am going to be a father, the day my first kid is born, the day I make a career change, holidays, or even the day I need to ask a question about how to fix something at my house. Those are the days where the knife stabbing my heart will go a little deeper as the wound opens again.

But the fact of the matter is I'm improving every single day, getting stronger and growing in the knowledge that my father loves me and is watching over me. To be honest, I don't think my father's loss will ever feel real to me. I lost of piece of myself that I won't get back until I see him again and get to hug him. Loss is something I'll have to deal with forever, but I get better each day at learning to cope and adapt.

I was raised by the best father who I loved beyond measure. This roller coaster ride of a healing process will yet have more peaks and valley, but I know the foundation of faith and love that my dad laid down will guide me through it all. I admired, respected, and honored my father. I aspired to be like him. Most importantly I loved my father more than anyone will understand. He is gone but will never be forgotten.

Be blessed,
James Brodie Speed

Chapter Twelve

FINDING MY NEW NORMAL

Shannon Owen

My biggest challenge since losing my dad in October of 2016 has been to find a sense of normalcy. I've learned that a major life disruption leaves its survivors with only pieces of life to put together in hopes of finding a new normal.

If I could go back in time I'd be more patient with myself, for I'm still working on feeling normal. I've learned recovery from trauma and loss isn't a fast process; at times it is frustrating. For me, the objective of healing isn't to go back to life as it once was because I know I'll never get there. Instead, I'm learning to embrace my own version of a new normal—complete with trauma, opportunities, and experiences (both good and bad)—with courage and patience.

My prayer is that sharing my personal experience on these pages will aid you in your own journey to wholeness or perhaps help you understand what someone else may be going through after losing a loved one in the line of duty.

Steve Owen came into my life when I was two years old. Three years later, in 1999, he married my mother. During the wedding ceremony Mom made vows to my two new brothers and Dad made vows to me, his new daughter. In part he said, "I promise to catch you whenever you may fall for the rest of your life and mine." He kept that promise until the day he died.

It takes a special kind of human being to take on becoming a stepparent (though that is not a term we used in our home). Being a dad is what Dad did best, other than being a great husband and a super cop. Dad became Dad not because my mom encouraged me to call him that, but because he earned the title. Our blended family wasn't perfect by any means; however, I never felt that my two brothers were treated differently than I. DNA does not make a family. What makes a family is the love, selflessness, and compassion members show each other.

I remember being a little girl, running after my dad down the hallways of the Lancaster Station, my backpack filled with drawing supplies, a couple of toys, and snacks. My brothers and I would sit at one of the empty desks at my dad's office and do our homework, draw, and annoy each other as we waited for Dad to finish his reports. This occurred most every week, so it's not surprising that Chadd, Tyler, and I thought of Lancaster Station as our second home.

One day I asked Dad about the photos of men and women in uniform that lined the hallway to his office. "Daddy, who are those people?"

He stopped, looked at the photos, and said, "They're deputies who were killed by bad guys. I worked with some of them."

I stood there for a moment studying the faces on the wall while Dad walked to his desk. I was too young to appreciate and understand the sacrifice made by those immortalized in the photos, and the impact their images must have had on their fellow officers who walked through the corridors of the Lancaster Station.

My parents were always honest with Chadd, Tyler, and me about the realities of their jobs in law enforcement. They told us there were evil people in the world and that anything could happen. Despite Mom and Dad's transparency about their jobs, I never thought we would lose a member of our family. I never thought I'd see the day when my dad's photo was mounted in that hallway.

But then October 5, 2016, happened.

On Thursday, October 13, the day of Dad's funeral, I was up at 5:00 a.m. feeling like death warmed over as I got dressed, applied makeup, and did my hair for the first time in over a week. I'd previously attended several funerals for members of law enforcement. I specifically recalled my parents riding their horses with the Los Angeles County Mounted Enforcement Detail at the funeral of Deputy David March, murdered during a traffic stop in Irwindale in April of 2002. I remembered a large number of law enforcement personnel being there, so I knew what to expect when we arrived at Lancaster Station to join the procession. Or so I thought.

I wasn't prepared for what I saw when we pulled up to the front of the station: patrol cars and motorcycles from departments across the nation packed the streets in every direction. Thousands of people lined the streets, and as we drove to the church I tried my best to read every banner and every shirt so thoughtfully created by members of our community.

I'd awakened that morning dreading the hours to come, for they would mark the reality that Dad wasn't coming back. He'd never again walk through the door after a shift to rummage through the fridge and pantry looking for a snack. Then, when he saw me, he'd smile and say, "What's up, Critter?" But as I peered through the window at the thousands of people, total strangers who couldn't see me through the tinted glass, I felt the comfort they brought that day. Peace officers and civilians together, the community mourned with our family.

The large church where we held Dad's services was packed, as was the overflow facility in a nearby building. I sat with my family on the front row as those closest to my dad eulogized him as a friend, coworker, sergeant, and—to many—a father figure who'd guided them in both their professional and personal lives.

As each member of our family took the podium to speak and my turn inched closer, I began to feel unsettled about what I'd chosen to talk about. Most people in the church that day thought Steve Owen was my biological father. We'd never corrected anyone when they assumed so. As I walked up to the pulpit I gathered myself, purposing to stick to what I'd written about the greatest gift that Dad had ever given me: a real dad.

I told the story of how my mom and biological father had shared 50/50 child custody until my seventeenth birthday when he decided to up and leave the state. My biological father's sudden departure had invoked an urgent question in my mind: would Dad have adopted me if he'd had the choice? It didn't take long to get the answer.

Riding home from school one day in my dad's patrol car I asked him point blank "Dad, if you'd had the chance to adopt me when I was younger, would you have done so?"

His perplexed expression was followed with a chuckle. "I don't need a piece of paper to tell me who my daughter is."

That was the end of the discussion. I'd been Dad's daughter since October 23, 1999, when his family of three became a family of five.

I ended my eulogy with what every person in the church now knew, saying, "He was my dad, my protector, the example of what a man, husband, and father should be. Ultimately, he was one of the greatest blessings in my life."

In early 2017 I began counseling with the department's therapist. I'd been hesitant at first, uncomfortable in exposing my loss and other parts of my life to a total stranger. Setting discomfort aside, I knew I needed help with issues that now occurred on a daily basis: nightmares, re-experiencing the event, and dealing with depression.

The Owens had always been a mostly private family; however, all sense of privacy was lost the day my dad was murdered. While the funeral, memorials, and subsequent events honoring Dad were astonishingly beautiful, they lacked the intimacy, peace, and comfort of being with only friends, family, and coworkers. In reality, the biggest trauma we'd ever experienced as a family was being broadcast to the public while the media, helicopters, cameras, and interviews came at us from every direction.

Although my choice to attend events honoring Dad reopened my wound, those events also brought great opportunities. I got to know people Dad worked with better, heard new stories about him, and built new friendships with deputies whom I now consider family. I now encourage those who've lost a loved one in the line of duty to remain or become close to their department members. Our blue line family has always been there for us, and I know they will continue to be.

I've learned that grief is a different experience for everyone, and there's no way of knowing how long it will take to overcome each of its aspects. Many are familiar with the five stages of grief: denial, anger, bargaining, depression, and acceptance. For me, they came in no particular order as I found myself bouncing between them depending on the day.

Faith played a major role in the grief process for most in the Owen family. I don't believe I would have made the progress I have with either counseling or faith alone. Though I'm a Christian, I didn't initially find much comfort in my faith following my dad's murder. I hadn't lost my faith; rather I was angry. Angry at the person who killed my dad, and angry at God. I wanted to know *why*—why my dad? Why leave my mom like this? Why cause such a disruption in my life and the lives of my family members?

I don't have the answers to those questions, but I do know my dad's death brought the following: People, many in law enforcement, came to Christ through Dad's life story. I met a number of amazing people who'd also lost loved ones in the line of duty, and we've had the opportunity to support each other. I am now fortunate enough to have multiple people in my life who understand faith, the loss of my dad and his death as a peace officer, and the struggle I've experienced with both.

My other issue as a Christian is that of forgiveness. I've neither forgiven the one who killed my dad nor am I prepared to do so any time soon. While my perspective differs from others in my family, I believe someone can only be forgiven if they express true remorse. In the case of my father's murder, the individual is not remorseful. If and when I decide to forgive his killer, I absolutely believe he should be held accountable and deserves the state's death penalty—forgiven or not.

A special man whom I feel deserves the most credit for helping me through the first few years following Dad's murder is my fiancé, Parker. Parker and I met during a ride-along (when a civilian spends a shift in the passenger seat with a member of law enforcement) on November 13, 2015.

I didn't find out until later that Dad had actually set up the ride-along in hopes Parker and I would start talking. In all honesty, I thought Parker was extremely awkward during our first few ride-alongs. Come to find out, he was terrified because I was Sergeant

Owen's daughter. He didn't want to be the guy who messed up with Sarge's daughter in the car.

Parker and I became friends as we continued our ride-alongs. Words can't describe how strong Parker was for me during those initial days and weeks following the murder while my family and I were being pulled in every direction. Parker and I started dating in December 2016.

Looking back, Parker and I never got to experience what I call the honeymoon phase of a new relationship that precedes a couple's becoming comfortable with each other. The aftermath of my dad's murder actually overtook our lives that first year together, and by January of 2018 I wasn't sure if the relationship would continue.

Though I'd been in counseling, I kept my thoughts about Dad's murder to myself. I reasoned that if I shared my thoughts with Parker he would think I had too many unresolved issues to be in a healthy relationship. The net result was that I was oftentimes moody towards him. If he asked what was going on my response was always "I don't want to talk about it." Finally, after about eighteen months, everything I'd been holding inside erupted—the bad, the worse, and the ugly.

I told Parker how hearing emergency sirens while I sat at a traffic light made my heart race. How sometimes, when I held Parker's hand, I could still feel Dad's cold hand and see his face riddled with bullet holes. I told Parker that each time I saw a patrol car, I'd peek over to see if it was my dad. And I told him how the sound of someone drinking through a straw made me think of the sound made when the nurses tried to clear the blood from Dad's airways. I explained that my daily life was plagued by these thoughts, and that I'd give anything to go through just one day without having them rob me of my peace.

I hadn't just lost my dad on October 5, 2016, I'd also lost him for all of my future birthdays and holidays, my wedding day, the birth of my children, and the random times throughout the day when I wanted to call him simply to hear his voice. I'd lost him for all the times still to come when I'd wish he were here. People talk about the weight of the badge, but these were lingerings of the badge my dad wore.

I'd poured out my heart to Parker, then it was his turn to speak. He told me how he wouldn't share with me when something was bothering him because of what I was already dealing with. He said, "There would be times when you'd be sad for no explainable reason. I knew there was a reason for the sadness, but I never knew what would trigger the dramatic outbursts. I felt helpless because I didn't know if the outburst was a result of something I said or did, or if it had to do with what appeared on TV or social media. At times I felt as if I were walking on eggshells when you were happy because I didn't want to accidentally cause you to become upset or sad. I was so frustrated in wanting to be there for you, yet I was unable to."

If that difficult discussion hadn't happened that night, I don't believe we would have proceeded with plans for our wedding. Parker and I agreed to go to counseling together, which made a world of difference in our relationship. As we learned to open up with each other, even about the bad things, our arguments became less frequent and eventually stopped. The change didn't happen overnight, but we both made a point to really fix our own issues for each other. Little did we know we were being prepared for another shooting.

The Sunday following Thanksgiving 2018 I was working my shift as a waitress in a local bar. I'd been there a few hours when I received several notifications on my Apple watch: "Is Parker okay?" "Hey, Parker good?" "Where are you and what about Parker?" I grabbed my phone from my pocket and read a text from Parker that simply said 998, code for "officer involved shooting."

I felt a lump in my throat and heard my heartbeat in my ears. My coworker asked what was wrong, but all I said was "Parker" before I disappeared out the back door to call him. I was worried when I got no answer, but not panicked. After all, he was able to text me that he'd been involved in a shooting. He was alive, but not knowing the nature of the incident brought emotions from two years ago to the surface. I punched in the numbers of other deputies, some my closest friends. Deputy Aaron Tanner picked up and said, "Hey Shannon, he's good—not injured. He's just talking to the sergeants right now, and when he's done I'll have him call you."

Aaron explained that Parker was the first to respond to a call about a man threatening his neighbors with a knife. When Parker arrived, the suspect was in the middle of the street wielding the knife, which Parker ordered him to drop. Instead, the suspect charged Parker with the knife, threatening to kill him. Parker had no choice but to shoot the man; however, the suspect lived.

My back against the outside wall of the building, I slid to the ground where I spent several minutes crying from both relief and sadness as the emotions from Dad's shooting flooded my soul. Parker's was the first deputy-involved Lancaster Station shooting since my dad was murdered.

Many think that as a daughter of a slain officer I'm not smart to choose a man in the same profession. Though some thought I would try to talk Parker out of being in law enforcement, I've never been overly concerned about him being a sheriff's deputy, even after the shooting he was involved in. I've never asked him to change the way he works or take positions that keep him out of the field. People have said, "It can happen to him too," but I choose not to live my life in fear. I love my fiancé and I know law enforcement is his calling. But that's not to say my dad's murder didn't reframe Parker's view of the job.

Parker had worked at the Lancaster Station three years when Dad was killed. He was in the field that day when the 998 traffic went out, and he responded with countless other officers to set up the containment to catch the suspect who'd shot my dad. I had called Parker on my way to the hospital to be with Dad but was unable to reach him. He later told me when he saw it was me calling, he couldn't bring himself to answer because he already knew how serious the situation was.

Parker and I have had numerous conversations about how Dad's murder affected him, which I asked him to share in his own words:

Experiencing Steve's death was the first time I had to face the reality of what I could ultimately sacrifice as a member of law enforcement. Before that day I'd read articles and had seen videos about officers being killed on the job. It was easy to say what I would have done differently and to pick apart their tactics. Like most officers, I had the idea in the back of my head that it would *never* be me in such a situation.

Besides, I couldn't be thinking about "that" when I was in the moment.

But Steve's murder was like a slap in the face for me. Here was a man considered by most to be the ultimate cop, larger than life, a true inspiration—yet he was murdered after answering a burglary call. It made me take a step back and realize that no matter how good I was or how well I trained and prepared both physically and mentally, the day could come when luck just wasn't on my side.

Losing Steve made me look at the world differently as well. As much as I love what I do, I don't want to do it 24/7. I don't want to max out on overtime, push the limit for that misdemeanor dope arrest, or run after the 417 suspect (person with a gun). I want to come home every night to my family and spend my days off with the people who matter most to me. Steve's death definitely rearranged the priorities in my life.

Law enforcement has always been, and will continue to be, a part of my life. I do not blame my dad's job for his death or Parker's shooting. Those in law enforcement have a calling on their lives. My dad loved police work, his community, and the people he worked with. If someone had told Dad that morning he wouldn't come home at the end of his shift, he'd still have put on his vest and walked out the door without disinclination. Truthfully, I know my dad would rather it be him that day than any of his brothers and sisters at the station. Dad is a hero because he rushed into danger, without a second thought, to help total strangers—just as he'd done for the past twenty-nine years. I couldn't be more proud as a daughter.

With both parents in law enforcement, the Owen home had three non-negotiable rules:

- Never leave the house angry.
- Never part without saying *I love you* to each other.
- Never give one-armed hugs.

Those values and traditions my dad taught me, along with the harsh realities and the "should haves" of his death, will help me navigate through marriage, motherhood, and life as a whole. My life experiences, both good and bad, have produced this realization: I've been blessed to have two amazing men in my life—my dad and my fiancé. Soon I am going to marry the man that *my hero* viewed to be of the same caliber. My eldest brother, Chadd, will walk me down the aisle in Dad's place to give away his little sister.

Finally, I'd like to leave you with a quote from the man I knew as my Uncle Mitch Speed. He spoke these words of comfort and wisdom to me following the death of my dad.

> As much as all this hurts, you have become stronger. Live each day truly understanding the fragility of life. Love those around you, knowing that nothing is promised beyond this day. God will use this pain and this experience to allow you to do incredible things in life and to help others—if you open up and allow Him to. There is no need to be angry,

because this is life. Hold on to the good times and appreciate everything you *do* have. As for all of us now, we will continue to walk this path together and we will continue to strengthen one another and love one another.

Chapter Thirteen

BLESSINGS IN THE MIDST OF TRIALS

Chadd Owen

At the time of this writing it has been almost four years since I lost my dad, Steve Owen. He was my hero.

Perhaps you too have lost a parent or someone close to you. If so, my prayer is that as you read this account of my personal journey you will find hope, encouragement, and love; that you will know you are not alone in life because I am in this battle just like you. My story will walk you through our family history, and how I survived the worst day of my life. I'll tell you what I learned as a result of this tragic experience and will give you some things to consider as we continue on this journey without our loved ones, in my case a father.

I grew up in Acton, California, in a Christian household of four: me, my brother, Mom, and Dad. I was seven years old when my parents divorced, and though I don't remember a lot about that time I do recall wanting my parents to be happy.

About three years later my dad married an amazing woman named Tania, and I gained a new mom and younger sister. Overall the five of us got along well, but we definitely had our differences and our share of fights. We all became better people through our shared new experiences and the key life lesson we learned together: you don't have to be blood to be family.

My dad worked a lot during those early years. During that time I remember him turning down two particular promotions—one to the SWAT team, the other to Sergeant—to ensure he could spend time with us and work close to home. He loved his job and worked a lot of overtime; however, he loved his family too. His overtime allowed us to have a lot of toys and go on family trips together.

We grew up with a motorhome, dirt bikes, and a boat. Dad was always so proud to take us on a three-week road trip each summer. Sometimes we went to the desert to ride dirt bikes, other times we went to Lake Powell to fish and water ski. We eventually saw most of the national parks located in the western United States; my childhood was definitely an adventure.

Dad was a volunteer coach for my football team from the time I was in the sixth grade until my freshman year of high school. He was also involved with the Sheriff Explorers program, which I went through at age fourteen. I was able to see and know Dad the cop, Dad the coach, and just Dad.

When I started playing football Dad taught me how to be a long snapper, a member of the special teams whose duty is to snap the football over a longer distance during punts, field goals, and extra points attempts. Not everyone has the ability to be a long snapper, a skill that can open the door to playing college football. Sure enough, I ended up being the long snapper at Upper Iowa University, where my brother, Tyler, joined me three years later and we enjoyed playing a year of football together. Dad and Tania flew out more times that I could count to watch our games.

After graduating from college I lived and worked in Iowa for the next four and a half years. But then I decided I didn't want to spend all of my vacation time going home to see family; I also wanted my future children to know their grandparents. I remembered my grandma coming to watch all of my childhood football games, and I wanted my kids to have similar opportunities. The only way that would happen was if I was back home in the Antelope Valley.

About a year after I moved back I went to work for Lockheed Martin, and met a beautiful woman named Nicole, who would become my wife. After Dad met her the first time he said, "Don't screw it up!" He was very happy when we got engaged, and even happier when we married on September 25, 2015.

Within a few months Nicole and I became dog parents to a yellow Labrador retriever puppy that we named Cooper. Three months later, when Dad, Tania, and Shannon came to our house for Christmas dinner, Dad let Cooper join him on the couch. I remember being so angry. I said, "Dad, you can't do that. He's not allowed on the couch!"

Dad just looked at me and said, "He can do whatever he wants. I'm Grandpa."

Little did I know that Christmas 2015 would be Dad's last. He would never have the chance to speak those words about my child.

October 5, 2016 started like any other day, other than Nicole and I were about to fly to Minnesota. Our family would join us in a couple of days for Tyler's upcoming graduation as a doctor of physical therapy, after which we would all attend the Vikings game together. Nicole and I left early to visit friends and watch the Upper Iowa game, or so we thought.

As Nicole and I prepared to board our flight at LAX I thought about texting Dad to let him know we were getting on the plane, but I chose not to because his response would likely be either "10-4" or "copy." The flight was smooth and without incident; however, within moments of landing in Minneapolis I got an ABC alert about a sergeant being shot in Lancaster. At the same time Nicole got a text from a friend that simply said, "I am so sorry!"

I texted Dad immediately and asked what had happened. I knew it couldn't be him, yet something didn't feel right. All of a sudden Tania called, and I felt one of my worst fears begin to unfold. I held the phone to my ear as Nicole and I pushed our way down the aisle with two hundred other people exiting the plane. I couldn't believe what I heard.

Tania told me Dad had been shot, but he was alive. She was about to be transported by helicopter back to Lancaster and said Nicole and I needed to get home as soon as possible. When we hung up I immediately began to pray as we made our way towards the terminal. My brother called, hysterical as he was leaving his apartment in Glendora to go to Lancaster. I told him to breathe and relax, that Dad may have been shot in the arm and didn't have his phone.

Tyler said he didn't think he could make it to Lancaster by himself, but I assured him he was strong and he *could* do it. I told him Nicole and I would be there as soon as possible. I found out later he had stopped at a California Highway Patrol station and was given a light-and-siren escort to Lancaster.

No sooner had I disconnected with Tyler than I got a call from a sergeant at the Lancaster Station. She said Dad had been shot and we needed to come home—the situation wasn't good. I pleaded with her to tell me where on his body he'd been shot. When she told me it was his face, I remember yelling "In the face?" as I stood in the middle of the Minneapolis airport.

I told Nicole what had happened and we went directly to the American Airlines counter for help in getting home. Several additional news updates that came across my phone confirmed the gravity of the situation. I told the agent at the counter about our situation and showed her the news reports on the phone confirming my dad had been shot. I handed her my credit card and said, "I don't care what it costs, we need to get home *now*."

God's grace showed up immediately. The agent told us her son was a police officer, and how sorry she was for what we were dealing with. She found two available seats next to each other on the next flight to LAX, which she gave us without charge. I called the Lancaster Station to tell the sergeant what time we'd arrive, and asked if they could arrange for a helicopter to take us to Lancaster. She said it was already covered.

As Nicole and I waited for our flight, Tania called again. She explained she was now at the Antelope Valley Hospital with Dad, and the situation didn't look good. As she described his physical condition it was as if my mind's eye saw what she saw. "Chadd, it doesn't look like he's going to make it. I'm going to put my phone next to his ear so that you can tell him goodbye."

I remember saying, "Dad, I am so proud of you. You've made me more than prepared for what our family is about to face—we'll have it from here. I love you and I will make you proud." I experienced comfort in the immediate situation as I felt God telling me everything was going to be okay.

Tania came back on the phone just as the agent announced it was time to board our flight. Because Nicole is a nurse she asked if she could speak to one of the nurses attending my dad. I did my best to hear what I could of the conversation as we boarded the plane and took our seats—something about a CT scan and performing CPR. Nicole handed the phone back to me, and I asked Tania to stay in touch via email for the duration of the flight. Then it was time to turn off our cell phones.

Nicole looked at me and said, "Chadd, the nurse told me they had performed CPR numerous times and could barely get him into a CT scan without losing him. You need to prepare yourself for your dad to pass."

BLESSINGS IN THE MIDST OF TRIALS

I began to bawl. The gentleman seated next to me overheard Nicole and I talking about getting connected to Wi-Fi and offered his login information. As it turned out, the man's father was a former LA Deputy who worked in the Antelope Valley. He had retired in the early 90s.

When I logged in and downloaded my email, I saw the worst two words I could have imagined: He's gone. I thought I was bawling before—now Nicole and I sat there holding each other, crying, and praying. The emptiness I felt at that moment remains indescribable, and there wasn't anything I could do about it. We were four hours away from LAX, so we began to text our family and friends to offer comfort from afar. We read every available news article in an effort to figure out what had happened. I continued my internal dialogue: *How could my dad have been killed? How can this be real?*

Later, as our plane began its descent into LAX, the captain announced that we had a family emergency and asked everyone to remain seated until we got off the plane. We stepped into the terminal and found a police escort waiting for us—every son and daughter's worst fear when growing up in a law enforcement family.

Every intersection between the airport and the location of the LASD helicopter was blocked so that we could get through without delay. On the flight to Lancaster, Nicole and I did our best to prepare ourselves for what we were about to see. When the helicopter landed we were greeted by one of my dad's closest friends along with our mothers. We all shed tears.

We were escorted to the room where our family and countless deputies sat with my dad's flag-draped body. I saw the blood on the flag and on his hands, his chest caved in from the ferocity of the

CPR. As I picked up the big, lifeless paw of my father's hand, I lost it again—how could he be gone?

We came together as a family and prayed that he didn't die in vain, that God would use this tragedy for His purpose. When it was time to escort Dad's body to the coroner's office, Nicole, Tyler, and his girlfriend rode together in a vehicle driven by one of the Lancaster Station deputies. Along the way to Los Angeles every overpass was filled with people saluting and paying tribute to my father.

I'd wondered how the community would respond to the tragic loss of a member of law enforcement, and now I knew. I was so proud to live in the Antelope Valley—and I still am.

Upon arrival in LA, deputies from Lancaster Station surrounded us as we escorted my dad into the receiving area, where we said our goodbyes. That was the last time we would see his body, and I'll always remember my final hug as if it were yesterday.

As a child I understood I would one day have to bury my dad, but I never imagined doing so at age twenty-seven. I drew strength from the knowledge that Dad was also twenty-seven when he lost his father.

I thought reality had set in that night at the coroner's office, but I was wrong. It was my dad's funeral that made his death so real. I'd been to several law enforcement funerals, but I was absolutely floored at the number of first responders in attendance at my dad's funeral. The expansive parking lot was filled with police cars from all over the country.

I was so nervous about giving the eulogy I'd prepared that I asked my wife to pray for me. God answered her prayer and the nervousness immediately disappeared. The service was absolutely beautiful, a great tribute to my father. Afterward Pastor Paul Chappell, who had officiated that day, told me how many people had been saved as a result of the message. I said, "That's great," and I meant it. However, I remember saying to myself *God can have them, but I want my dad back. Why did Dad have to die for so many people to be saved?*

I knew life was going to be different moving forward. The amazing support that surrounded us would gradually diminish as most people returned to their daily lives, yet we would continue to mourn. That's just how life works.

In the weeks that followed I experienced grief and bitterness. I was upset with God and began to question how He could have let this happen. Why did my dad have to go? Why was he executed?

As I continued to pray about the matter and study my Bible, something happened. I found that both scripture verses and the idea of heaven were more real to me. Heaven wasn't merely some ethereal place where Christians go when their lives on earth are done. I realized heaven was a real place—the place where my father now existed.

The Bible speaks of a time when God will pour out His Spirit, saying *Your young men shall see visions* (Acts 2:17), so I wasn't surprised when I had a vision of heaven. In the vision I was in heaven and saw both Jesus and my dad. I was so happy to see my dad that I walked right past Jesus and straight to my father's arms.

Later, when I told Nicole about the vision and bypassing Jesus, she reassured me that my actions made sense based on the fact that I'd just suffered a traumatic loss. She encouraged me to give myself time to sort out my feelings, and to see what God revealed to me about the meaning of the vision.

As I contemplated the vision I soon understood it's meaning: it is *because* Jesus is our Savior we have the opportunity to see our loved ones again. As I continued to meditate on the vision my thoughts of heaven began to strengthen and shape my faith.

For example, I was talking to my father-in-law one day about the particularly difficult time I was having with missing my dad. He said, "Chadd, do you think that after spending time in heaven your dad would want to come back to earth?"

I didn't hesitate for a second. "Absolutely not!" I have since learned to use the vision God gave me of heaven as a tool to keep my spirits up. Now, each time I envision my dad in heaven, I smile.

Nicole and I did our best to continue doing the things we enjoyed, including going to UCLA football games and (for me) hunting. Dad and I had always loved hunting together; in fact, the last day I spent with him we were getting ready for hunting season.

Due to the public nature of my father's death, it seemed there was some sort of event to honor his life on a weekly basis. Nicole and I felt that our presence at these events, showing our strength, would help point others to Christ. We'd celebrated our first wedding anniversary only ten days before my dad died, so we were still a young married couple. Oftentimes when we ran into people we knew, it was clear they didn't know what to say to us, or how to offer comfort. I'm not sure there is anything to say other than we are sorry for your loss and are praying for you.

Sometimes when Nicole and I were out together we'd notice people staring at us and whispering. They'd likely recognized us as members of the Owen family from the yet unending media reports. With so much public attention and so many events to attend, I fought to maintain balance between my responsibilities as a husband and the public spotlight. I'm thankful Nicole helped me prioritize my life in a way that ensured the health of our marriage.

I also fought to find my new normal—a new normal without Dad. At times it felt as if I'd take two steps forward and then something would trigger me into taking a giant step backwards. Each event that honored my father would again open up a wound that I so desperately wanted to become a scar. I knew Dad would want me on a life track filled with happiness and joy. The last thing he would want for any member of our family would be to feel down or upset. One of his favorite things to tell us was, "Quit your wee-weeing!"

Several events we attended as a family were particularly comforting. One was the California Peace Officers Memorial Ceremonies, the other National Police Week in Washington DC. In both instances it was great to sit with other survivors, the term coined for those who'd lost loved ones in the line of duty. It was there I realized we weren't the only children who'd lost parents. Though we were all struggling, we could lean on each other for strength.

Nicole and I noticed the first shift towards normalcy following the trip to Washington DC. As the events slowed down, we felt as if we were getting our lives back. We purchased a travel trailer and began camping together. Not only was camping a great childhood memory for me, it's also been a fruitful experience for our marriage.

Before I knew it the one-year anniversary of my dad's death was upon us. Sure enough, October 5, 2017, brought back all of the memories and emotions that had been so raw and painful just twelve months earlier. But we also had another matter to deal with; that being attending court appearances by the suspect accused of murdering my father. I especially remember how seeing him at the first hearing took all of my physical, emotional, and spiritual strength.

Though I didn't realize it at first, those court hearings opened the door to another battle that I'd known all along was coming. It was the battle over *forgiveness.*

Someone asked me, "Chadd, if your dad's killer accepted Christ could the two of them be friends in heaven?" I couldn't imagine the idea and, quite honestly, the question hurt me.

In my mind the man didn't deserve forgiveness—he'd deliberately killed my dad! Needless to say, I harbored a lot of anger towards my dad's killer. I had my own ideas of how he should be punished, none of which are appropriate to mention here. Neither a sentence of life in prison nor of death was good enough, but at the end of the day I knew those were the only legal options.

Though I'd given my dad's death to God a while back knowing I couldn't walk this path alone, I'd not yet forgiven the killer. One night as I read my daily devotion this verse jumped out at me: *"But if you refuse to forgive others, your Father will not forgive your sins*" (Matthew 6:15 NLT). Then I backed up to verse 14: *"If you forgive those who sin against you, your heavenly Father will forgive you."* These weren't the words of Matthew—these were Jesus' words! Well, I don't think God could have made it any clearer than that. If I wanted God to forgive me, I had to forgive my dad's killer.

As humans (including Christians) we tend to rank sin according to how we view the severity of its outcome. Society plays a big part in how we view various kinds of sin. The Bible says, *For the commandments, "You shall not commit adultery," "You shall not murder," "You shall not steal," "You shall not bear false witness," "You shall not covet," and if there is any other commandment, are all summed up in this saying, namely, "You shall love your neighbor as yourself"* (Romans 13:9).

Romans 12:19 (EHV) states *Do not take revenge, dear friends, but leave room for God's wrath. For it is written, "Vengeance is mine; I will repay," says the Lord.* These verses made me realize that sin is sin, and we are all on a level playing field. I needed to stop judging and start loving. I knew God wanted me to forgive the man who'd been responsible for taking my father away.

When it was time for the preliminary hearing to begin I had the opportunity to meet the suspect's family, but I turned it down because I wasn't ready. I hadn't forgiven the suspect and I wasn't ready to do so. But as I continued to meditate on the verses of scripture I'd read in the book of Romans, I saw I was actually judging the suspect's family by his actions. His family didn't make him pull the trigger; he made that decision on his own. I was judging his family when, in fact, they probably needed love as much as our family did. These thoughts ate at me for a few weeks until finally I made my own decision: I chose to forgive the suspect. And when I did—wow! The burden I'd carried lifted immediately from my shoulders.

My forgiving the suspect didn't erase the scar on my heart from losing my dad, nor has it prevented that scar from getting nicked from time to time. Some of the hardest times I've experienced came following the birth of my son. I wish so much my dad were here to hold his grandson. I know he would smile from ear to ear. My job as a father is to make sure my son knows the man his grandpa was. The lessons I teach my son through this experience will help carry him through his life. My duty is to prepare my son for life just as my father prepared me—and as our heavenly Father prepared us. I take peace in knowing my son will forever have a guardian angel.

God has a plan for each one of us, and the grace He gives to accompany that plan is unfathomable. When we mess things up and don't have our priorities right, God is abundant in His forgiveness. The Bible says, *"Therefore know that the LORD your God, He is God, the faithful God who keeps covenant and mercy for a thousand generations with those who love Him and keep His commandments"* (Deuteronomy 7:9). Looking back, I now see that I hadn't fully grasped God's mercy, forgiveness, and love until I went through that tragic experience. I still have a lot to learn, but as a Christian I am to set the example when it comes to exhibiting God's love, grace, and forgiveness.

It's easy to get wrapped up in the nuances of day-to-day life. I used to get frustrated with people who were rude or drove too fast on the freeway. I'm in no way condoning reckless driving, but I've learned to consider the pain or sorrow others may be experiencing. Perhaps those who don't behave as we wish they would are having a bad day. Maybe a family member is in the hospital or, worse, they may have just lost the person they loved the most. We've all needed mercy when we didn't deserve it; therefore, we should be willing to extend that mercy to others.

If I had to choose a verse to encourage me (and you) through a rough time or a difficult trial it would be James 1:2–4: *My brethren, count it all joy when you fall into various trials, knowing that the testing of your faith produces patience. But let patience have its perfect work, that you may be perfect and complete, lacking nothing.* Notice this verse doesn't say trials are a joy; rather, we are to consider our falling into those trials joy.

No matter the trial we run or walk through, I believe God will bless us in the trial if we are only willing to see His blessing. Walking through the trial of losing my father gave me opportunities to sit down and witness to friends and coworkers. When asked how I made it through the horror of his murder, I simply pointed them to the Man upstairs. In those moments I communicated silently with Him saying *Okay God, I see what You are doing and I see how you are using me.* Those special times always brought a smile to my face.

Looking again at James 1:2–4 we see the result of our patience is that we are made "perfect and complete, lacking nothing." I'm still a work in progress, but I give a lot of credit for that progress to the man I called my "new dad on earth" following the loss of my father.

That man was Mitch Speed, who really stepped up to the plate for me (and my siblings). I spent many hours with Mitch, who was willing to give me a helping hand despite his battle with cancer. He encouraged me and challenged me to live my life to the fullest, to love Christ more each day. I still hear Mitch in my head anytime

I'm tempted to worry about something: "Chadd, if you are still worrying then you haven't fully given the matter to God." Mitch was another great leader who went home too soon but, just like my dad, I know he wouldn't want to come back to this life.

My point is this: blessings occur in our lives even in the midst of the most horrific of trials—if we are willing to see them. God is always here for us. If we ask Him to see the good in even the worst of situations (for me it was the loss of my father), He will most certainly show us.

In closing, contributing to this amazing book and allowing you to read my story is yet another blessing on my life following the loss of my father. If I can help just one person, it's the least I can do. After all, that's exactly what members of law enforcement do each and every day, knowing full well the potential consequences of their service to their communities.

God's blessings are everywhere. We just have to ask Him to give us the vision to see them.

I'd like to leave you with something to ponder, which has really helped me let go of a lot of anger. I used to envision going to heaven and asking God why He took my dad, why we had to lose him so soon. But the more I spent time in the presence of Jesus that vision began to change. I realized that if I'm going to spend eternity with Jesus Christ—and my dad—does it really matter that I lost out on spending thirty years with him here on earth? I also understand that any harm or wrong we've experienced in this life will not exist in heaven. That's why I encourage you to do as I've done. Give all of your pain and sorrow to God *now*, knowing that eternal perfection awaits in heaven.

BLESSINGS IN THE MIDST OF TRIALS

Be anxious for nothing, but in everything by prayer and supplication, with thanksgiving, let your requests be made known to God; and the peace of God, which surpasses all understanding, will guard your hearts and minds through Christ Jesus.

PHILIPPIANS 4:6-7

Epilogue

TANIA AND VICKIE

In January 2019 we received an invitation to share our story and testimony at an outreach event in front of a live audience of first responders.

Having never made a presentation together, we were at first a bit apprehensive about speaking to a live audience, but we decided if we could help just one marriage, then our speaking to the group would be well worth it. As we prepared to deliver our first message, we found a Bible verse that encouraged us, in which Jesus said, *"Do not worry beforehand, or premeditate what you will speak. But whatever is given you in that hour, speak that; for it is not you who speak, but the Holy Spirit"* (Mark 13:11).

When the day of the event arrived, we had no idea if we would speak to ten people or a hundred. To our surprise the auditorium was packed with over five hundred first responders and spouses who welcomed us with open hearts. We spoke for five hours, sharing our individual stories in total transparency, holding nothing back. During that time we alternately laughed and cried together with our audience, but in the end we were all strengthened and affirmed as members of one unique community and calling.

In that initial event we covered five specific topics.

One: Home needs to be a safe place. Whether our loved ones chase bad guys, put out fires, or bring first-response help and comfort in times of trauma, they all need a safe place where they can shut out the intense activity encountered on a daily basis. When Vickie shared with Mitch the fact that she resented his job and why, it was she who came away from the conversation enlightened. Their home was the only place he could come to shut down. It was the place where he could lock the doors and put his gun away. He didn't have to look over his shoulder to see who might be chasing him. Instead he could lie down on the sofa and watch TV without worry. Home should always be a haven for our first responders.

Two: Spouses need to listen. Though the need to listen better to one's spouse is a common issue in many marriages, it is a critical issue in first-responder marriages. Human beings are not all alike—personalities and emotional qualities are unique to each individual. For many first responders, talking about the events of their day is a way to decompress. They aren't looking for feedback. Rather, they just need someone to listen. If we don't take the time to listen to our spouses, somebody else will. This is one of the reasons divorce rates are so high among first-responder marriages.

Three: Women, we are stronger than we think. One thing the two of us have learned is just how powerful women are in the home.

God gave men wonderful physical strength, but He gave women the kind of strength that makes us the glue that holds our homes together. Being strong for our husbands means providing a place where they can be vulnerable, thus giving them a place to rest their heads in an atmosphere of trust. It takes trust to develop the kind of closeness and love that brings a couple together as God intended—and He gave us the strength to do it.

Four: Make boyfriend-girlfriend time together. Let's face it, men are first attracted to us physically, and then they fall in love with our hearts. Remember how much fun it was when we were courting, when we went out of our way to look good for our future husband? When both the man and woman did all they could to please each other? Sadly, once a couple is married, they lose the wonder of being boyfriend-girlfriend as life and child rearing take over. But the good news is we can *choose* to make time to date each other. One piece of advice Tania always gives young wives is this: No granny panties! Don't ever wear granny panties to bed—always look your best for your husband.

Five: Put God first in your marriage. We can neither maintain a good marriage nor heal a broken one without putting God first—this is true of *all* marriages. After all, God created marriage to be a blessing, for the Bible says, *Therefore a man shall leave his father and mother and be joined to his wife, and they shall become one flesh* (Genesis 2:24). As women we are created to love and honor our husbands. The two of us were amazed at what happened when we stopped trying to change our husbands and instead focused on changing ourselves. As a result, God healed our marriages and gave us the most wonderful ever, love-filled final years with our husbands before they went home to be with the Lord.

Though we are both blessed to have experienced the kind of love that comes from being married to godly husbands, we've also experienced tragedy and loss in our marriages. We firmly believe God has called us to share our stories to help other law-enforcement families as well as all first-responder families.

That's why we've decided to write a second book to be titled *Lessons from the Badge*. In it we will detail what we learned after walking through the dark days of our marriages and—more importantly—the changes God led us to make as we cooperated with Him in the healing and restoration of our marriages. You can check our website, VickieandTania.com, for updates on our progress and the release date.

In the meantime, we pray God's blessing and favor over you and your family.

Bonus Content

POEM AND ESSAY BY MITCH SPEED

"Therefore every scribe instructed concerning the kingdom of heaven is like a householder who brings out his treasure things new and old."

MATTHEW 13:52

DEATH

A poem by Mitch Speed
March 1983

Death is not merely a word
Or a concept only imagined.
Death is a reality far more realistic
Than today's society tends to think.

Death can come as a sudden tragedy
Or a long-awaited guest.
Death should not be thought of as
A cruel or gruesome part of life.

Death is not an end to one's life.
Death is a birth into the real life
that we should worry about.
Physical life on earth is nothing more
Than a preparation, a practice run for
what is to come after death.

We should not be drug down with sorrows
Over the loss of a loved one.
Death should be looked upon as a new birth,
A new beginning for those that pass away.

YOUR FINAL THIRTY MINUTES

An essay by Mitch Speed

Lend me your imagination if you would.

You are ten years old. You are with your parents at a friend's house. Your mother and father are downstairs while you and your friend are upstairs playing.

You have been playing for hours and have been having a great time. These are your best friends, and you always enjoy the time you get to spend with them. Time always seems to pass much too quickly while you are with them, and you are constantly aware of that fact that you will have to leave in a while.

It's late in the evening, and you hear your father's footsteps as he is coming up the stairs. You open the bedroom door and see your father standing there. Much to your dismay, he tells you it will be time to go home in about thirty minutes. He tells you to gather your toys and start getting ready to leave. Even though you have been enjoying yourself for hours, you begin to plead with him to give you a little more time. He tells you that you can play a little longer, but you need to be ready to go soon.

You beg and plead with your father to let you stay the night. Your father says no. You look at your friend, silently begging for him to say something, but he already knows the answer will be no. You fold your arms across your chest, as if that is really going to help matters, and turn away from your father. You are angry and feeling a bit ungrateful.

Your father goes back downstairs and you literally start having a fit since you don't want to go home. You need to come up with a plan for your father to let you stay longer or spend the night. Your best friend tries to calm you down by reminding you that you still have time to finish the game you are playing. You are so upset that you can't even concentrate on your game, even though you were having the time of your life five minutes earlier.

You look out the window as you tell your friend, "This isn't fair!" You were having so much fun, and now you must leave! What's the point in even playing? As soon as you start to have fun it's always time to leave! You complain that you might as well have stayed home. You spend your last thirty minutes in a tizzy because you don't want to go home.

Your father calls out to you and you drag yourself downstairs and leave, miserable. You have successfully wasted your final thirty minutes of fun you could have had with your friend. You leave, so upset that you don't even tell your friends goodbye.

Sound familiar?

I know I played out that scenario many times as a child. Wasting my final thirty minutes throwing a fit because I didn't want to leave.

Now let's apply this same scenario to our life as adults.

I have chosen to look at my cancer diagnosis much in the same way. My life has been incredible! God has blessed me with a lifetime full of love and enjoyment. And now, at the age of fifty-two, God has knocked on the door and told me that it's almost time to go home. No arguing or pleading is going to change the fact that He will eventually call us all home. Should I be bitter? Should I forget about all the wonderful years He has blessed me with? Should I fold my arms across my chest and stare out the window, upset that my time is approaching? I say *no*!

As children, we had the choice to spend our final thirty minutes playing or to spend them pouting. As adults, we have the choice to spend our final thirty minutes living or spend them dying. It's really that simple.

I don't know how long I have left, but I do know the clock is ticking. I may have thirty more years or thirty more minutes. But I am well aware that God has tapped me on the shoulder and said, "Be ready my son."

So, I am choosing to live! I have chosen to spend my final thirty minutes with a thankful heart and a smile on my face. I have made the decision to express my love for those in my life. I am thankful that God blessed me with such a wonderful life! I have the most incredible wife and son that any man could ever ask for. Each day they make me smile and fill my heart with pride. And it is my responsibility to show my family and friends how thankful I am to have them in my life. I need to set the example and prepare those who will join me some day in heaven.

Please don't read anything into this because I plan on hanging around for a long time. But quite honestly, only God knows how long I have. Only God knows how long you have. Can we cherish our time together? Can we live life to the fullest and understand that each day is a blessing? Can we agree to disagree about the little differences we have? Can we just love one another and enjoy each other's company?

God, thank You for all You have blessed me with. Thank You for opening my eyes and my ears to all You have bestowed upon me. Thank You for my wife, my son, my family, and my friends. Use me, Lord, in whatever way You see fit so that I may fulfill Your wishes. You really are too good to me.

When my time is officially over here on earth, I want to leave a legacy of love and strength through my faith in our God. I want to leave you the same legacy my mother left for me. She prepared me for this season in my life, and I am a thankful man.

Look at yourself in the mirror, right now, and decide what you want to do with your final thirty minutes. It really is that simple.

Now excuse me while I go on living.

ALSO FROM OWEN-SPEED PUBLISHERS

DETECTIVE MITCH SPEED served with the Los Angeles County Sheriff's Department for sixteen years, during which time he was publicly recognized as representing "the best of law enforcement in terms of respect for citizens, respect for his community, and a commitment to exemplary service above all else."

In his personal life Mitch was esteemed as a loving husband, father, mentor, and worship leader committed to helping others and serving God. After being diagnosed in 2016 with stage-4 cancer, Mitch spent countless hours in front of his computer penning a book initially intended for family and friends. However, since its original release in 2017, ***Mitch Speed—The Man Behind the Badge*** has been reprinted multiple times after finding its way into the hands and hearts of Americans of all walks of life.

This second edition features all the original cherished stories and poetry of cowboy-cop philosopher Mitch Speed. It also includes messages from Vickie Speed and Brodie Speed, Mitch's wife and son, as well as additional content discovered posthumously on his computer.

And now, we welcome you to the ever-growing number of "Speed Readers" blessed to spend time with the inspiring and soul-nurturing words of Mitch Speed, the man behind the badge.

ACKNOWLEDGEMENTS

It took an army of incredible people to get this book done. Most don't even know the roll they played in our lives or the strength they gave our families.

To Los Angeles County Sheriff's Department, Sheriff Jim McDonnell: Thank you for being there from the moment Steve was murdered, being present while Mitch was fighting cancer, and carrying our families through an incredibly emotional and difficult time.

To the Los Angeles County Sheriff's Department Special Enforcement Bureau and Bomb Squad; Los Angeles County Sheriff's Department, Lancaster Station; Lancaster Station, LAN-CAP Team and Detective Bureau: Thank you from the bottom of our hearts for being partners and family, and for loving us through loss and tragedy.

To Los Angeles County Sheriff's Department Detective Mike Markman: You have been the protector and keeper of the Owen family. You were Steve's right hand, and he knew the quality of man that served and protected by his side.

To Steve's team: The Owen family holds strong because you walk by our side and have never left us. Thank you for keeping Steve's memory alive.

To Los Angeles County Sheriff's Department Sergeant Theresa Dawson (from Tania): You were the glue that held everything together. You were my sister, partner, driver, escort officer, and woman in charge. You were truly an amazing blessing to both families.

To Los Angeles County Sheriff's Department Sergeant Troy Bowser of the Detective Bureau; Detectives Kessee, Mahoney, Grajalva, Tanner, Gore, McNutt, Vesna (and the many not listed) and retired Deputy Chatman (from Vickie): Your never-ending support to Mitch as he be battled cancer and the care you take of the Speed family has no words.

To Kelly's Irish Times, Sergeant John Krupinsky (the best host): We are grateful for the men and women in blue and the bond that was strengthened between us and them. It was during this time in 2019 that our (Tania and Vickie) friendship turned into a sisterhood. Our bond with two great men, that even though we are thousands of miles apart, have encouraged and supported us to keep the course Your friendship, conversations (BDE) and laughter have made the tough days better and kept a Cali Girl stronger than she thought.

To The Road Church of the AV, leaders John and Darlene Santero, Jason and Miriam Grundy, and the worship team: For the love of our church family during the loss of two incredible men and your continued prayers as we push forward in God's calling on our lives, we thank you.

To Lancaster Baptist Church Pastor Paul Chappell and The Highlands Church of Palmdale Pastor Mark Goodell: Thank you for being great leaders in our community and a strong voice for law enforcement.

To the Lancaster City Council: We are grateful for your dedication to The Lancaster Sheriff Station and your love for our husbands and the community.

To the community of Lancaster, California: We cannot express enough gratitude for the love and support from complete strangers who honored two men who protected and served this great city.

To our family and friends: Your love and support have gotten us through some really tough days and have encouraged us to keep pushing hard for this calling we have on our lives.

To our editor and book producer, Stacie Jennings, and her amazing husband, Mark Imboden: No words can express the blessings you have brought to our lives. You took on a project by faith and made this book more than we could have ever imagined. You both have loved us, prayed for us, and taken us in as family—and that we are, family.

Most importantly is our heavenly Father: Without Your love, patience, and strength we would not be standing. You have taken two women whose lives were shattered and filled with pain and given us purpose to serve others and truly make a positive change in the world. Only our God is loving enough to use two of the most unusable women.

CPSIA information can be obtained
at www.ICGtesting.com
Printed in the USA
FSHW020647140621
82358FS